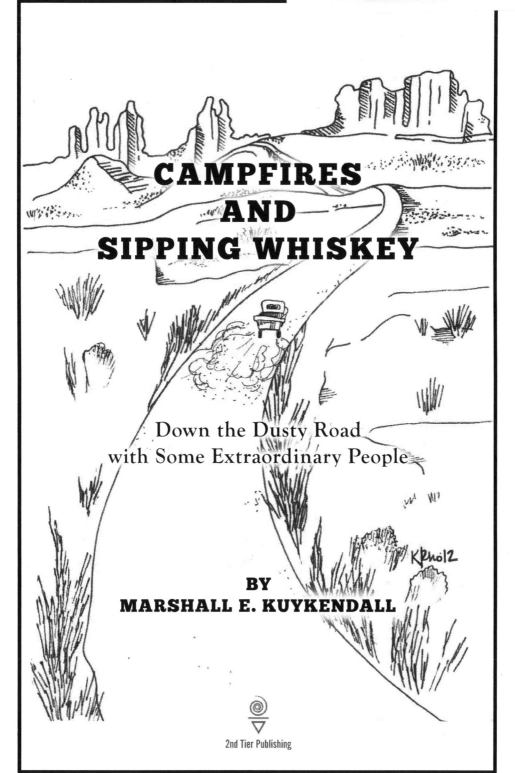

# CAMPFIRES AND SIPPING WHISKEY

## Down the Dusty Road
## with Some Extraordinary People

### BY
### MARSHALL E. KUYKENDALL

2nd Tier Publishing

Published by:
    2nd Tier Publishing
    501 Wimberley Oaks Dr
    Wimberley, TX 78676

ISBN 978-0-578-11617-4

Project managed by Courtney Donnell
Cover photograph and book design by Dan Gauthier

To Betty,
the love of my life.
Without a doubt
the most "extraordinary person"
I have ever met.

Who ever it was sitting around lamenting that
"Into everyone's life a little rain must fall"
never lived on a ranch in the desert southwest.

—MEK

# CONTENTS

# PREFACE

I never say that the Old Times were better. They weren't; just different. Here are some people and places in my life that I need to write about before the memory sneaks away into some hidden place where neither God nor beast can find it. Not everyone is as fortunate as I am to have been born on a big ranch in Texas before things got too fancy and the electric lights had not been turned on yet.

Let's head down that dusty road and see who we can find!

# FORWARD

## John Jefferson

This book, the fourth by Marshall Kuykendall, will introduce readers to some characters you've never heard of but will wish you had known, as he has, and let you in on some things about well-known personalities that other historians might have missed.

There is mirth throughout most of the book—a lot of it—and a little irony, at times. He wrote about Texas Ranger Captain Frank Hamer and the captain's several visits to the Kuykendall's ranch. Hamer and Marshall's father, Bill Kuykendall, were friends, and from what I know about each of them, it's not surprising. The two adults would sit on the front porch of the ranch sharing tales while young Marshall would be sequestered in his room, reading about gun fighters of the old West. From the bullet and shotgun wounds Captain Hamer carried to his grave—not to mention the hombres he sent to theirs, including the infamous Bonnie Parker and Clyde Barrow—the colorful Ranger Captain merits his own place among gun fighter lore. Think what Marshall missed; he could have read later.

To term the people Marshall has written about in *Campfires and Sipping Whiskey* as *colorful* is as understated as saying John M. Browning and Samuel Colt were *inventors*.

He wrote almost poetically about campfire companions and hunting adventures near Marfa, in South Texas, in Old and New Mexico, and in Colorado and Wyoming. But don't think this is a book about *Marshall*, the hero. Much of it is self-deprecating and his cast of characters doesn't always get its buck. He wrote it to share some of the lively, occasionally outrageous people he has run with throughout a fertile, rawhide life lived mostly in the outdoors. It is rich in the heritage of independent, stalwart, sometimes rambunctious men who were - in their own right—Texas pioneers of the 1900s.

Some of his cohorts—like radio and television personality, Cactus Pryor, or Audie Murphy, the most decorated American soldier in history—were well-known. Others—like Bill Peace and "Uncle Bear"—might have endured eternity in peaceful obscurity had not Marshall brought them to life on these pages.

The only common denominator among Marshall's subjects was that they were the men in his life whose friendships he cherished—some for their accomplishments, but much more because they helped mold Marshall's own unapologetic brand of Texas individualism.

They are the ones who endowed him with the spirit to start a landowner revolution in the early 1990s against oppressive interference by a federal agency. That meant he had to state his case to leaders in the Capitol and that led to a confrontation with then Lieutenant Governor Bob Bullock—the meanest S.O.B. in the valley of state government. Bullock called Marshall and was berating him for clogging his and Governor Ann Richards' fax machines with "Take Back Texas" messages. Marshall's unflinching reply was, "Mr. Bullock, I didn't paint that bull's-eye on her ass."

Bullock hooted at that loudly enough to be heard all the way across the lawn to the Governor's Mansion. But he threw his support behind "Take Back Texas," and landowner rights fought back the federal invaders.

Marshall Kuykendall writes—as he speaks—with the hair left on. The book is a good read ...and a great ride!

— *John Jefferson*, Outdoor Writer
Austin, Texas

Always carry a flagon of whiskey
in case of snakebite and furthermore,
always carry a small snake.

—W. C. Fields

David LaVern Allen

# David LaVern Allen
## Kyle, Texas

David LaVern and I have been friends and close neighbors our whole lives. He was born and raised on a ranch on the Blanco River just west of Kyle and I was born and raised on a ranch on Onion Creek just northwest of there. His father, LaVern, and my father were life-long friends as far back as I can remember. I have photos of the two of them together from the 1930s and 40s riding on the 101 Kuykendall ranch and hunting together in the 1940s in and around Cotulla, Texas.

David's mother, Grace, was a Nance from a very old central Texas ranching family; her sister was married to Dudley Story Sr. from Cotulla. I vaguely remember David coming up to our ranch back in the 30s. But we didn't get together full time until the fall of 1948 when we moved to the south side of the 101 Ranch and I transferred into the school system at Kyle where David went to school.

In those years the population of Kyle was only 2–300 and there were very few kids going to school there. When I entered my junior year at Kyle High School there were only about 8 or 10 students per class, hard to imagine by today's standards.

## Six Man Football

One thing about being in a small school like Kyle, you participated in everything and every sport. You had to. The school desperately needed every warm body it could muster to play all the sports on the schedule or the school system would suffer.

I don't remember everyone in my class, but I do remember David LaVern and Edward Schmeltekopf, of the Schmeltekopf clan. Every boy was required to go out for football. If you didn't, your family was blacklisted forever. There were only about 10-12 boys in all of the high school grades and if you had blood in your body, your butt was on the team, whether you liked it or not. There were not enough students in the district to play regular eleven man football, so our district played six man football and man, it was fast and rough.

We were a lot smaller in those years. I know; sounds crazy doesn't it? But in 1948 I was 16, stood about 5-4 and probably weighed about 125 pounds. David LaVern and Arthur were both about 5-8 and probably weighed slightly more. I remember that Ann Miller was in my class and she was 5-8 and I had to look up at her. I also know that by the end of my senior year I was taller than she was, different times. Now a'days, high school kids are 6-4 and weigh 250 pounds; must have been the introduction of the Wheaties.

**1949 Kyle Panthers**

Our football coach that year was a man named Black and he tried to kill us, or at least I thought that was what he was doing. We started football practice in early August that year when it was about 100 degrees. There were barely enough uniforms to go around, and none of them fit. Mine hung on me like an old wool sack and the sweat in it still had that wonderful aroma from seasons passed that I couldn't quite place, no matter how many times it had been cleaned.

Kyle High School really didn't have a football field as such but an open space behind the school that was probably plowed for cotton in the off season and then drug smooth in the fall of the year for football. At least, that is what it felt like. I remember before the first game we ever played, all the men in the bleachers got out and walked up and down the field, throwing off all the bigger rocks they could find.

David was the quarter back for the team and he was tough as a cedar stump. In those years since there were so few kids, everyone played both offense and defense. So everyone played both sides of the line. I would have never gotten to play if Jack Peoples hadn't gotten his leg broken plumb off in the second or third game of the season. All I remember was Jack was laying east and west and his leg was laying north and south. They used a hook and a team of horses to pull him from the playing field. Kinda reminded me of the glory days of The Coliseum when all was for King and Country or was it for Caesar? I can't remember that far back.

David had a 36 Ford Model T pickup that he drove to school every day. I thought that was just about the best thing I had ever seen. We became best buddies and he let me ride in it as long as I wouldn't turn the key off. The reason I say that is because I did turn it off one day and when I turned it back on the backfire blew the muffler completely off the car. David was a tad miffed over that.

David was the most popular person in our senior class and was voted the "One Most Likely to Succeed." I was proud to note that I was voted the "One Most Likely To" but to what, no one ever told me. But I will tell you this, I graduated 9th in my senior class and how many of you can atone to that distinction? So there!

## The Graduation Trip

We graduated in the spring of 1950. David, Edward and I decided to take our senior trip by driving my 48 Jeepster 4-cylinder car all the way to Canada and back in 10 days. It got great gas mileage, but who cared in those days. It ran about 48 miles per hour on the straight-away and about 59 per hour on any really steep downhill parts of the road. We made a state a day; all the way to Canada, roared across Montana into Alberta, Canada; took a picture of the Canadian flag, came roaring back across the US border only to be stopped by US Customs wanting to know what in the hell we were doing in Canada. We weren't in to cussing in those days, that came later, but we thought, "What the shit?" We crossed in front of the idiots in a gigantic grass plain that covered about one million acres, drove right under the American flag; drove over to the Canadian flag pole, took a damn picture and drove back. What is so complicated about that? Well, let me tell you, rules are rules. Oh, well.

One funny thing we noticed, as we drove further and further north, the breakfasts got bigger and bigger and bigger. I mean, in Clovis, NM we had a taco; in Steamboat Springs, Colorado, we had two eggs and a pancake; in Jackson Hole, Wyoming, we had two eggs, two pancakes and hash-browns. By the time we got into Glacier National Park, we had two eggs, nine pancakes and a steak.

What we liked about the Montana pancakes, was, you could lean out the window of our speeding vehicle and sail them like a Frisbee out plumb across any mountain valley and the suckers would go a mile. Of course, that was before Frisbees were invented.

In those days, you got your money changed into paper bills or silver dollars. Folks out west were big into silver dollars. We had a one gallon water thermos and maybe $400 between us so we hit upon the idea to change all our money into silver dollars and hide them in the thermos. Damn thing weighed about 35 pounds, but who would have guessed where our stash was hidden? No one!

We got home with about half of them and Dad thought that was just about the dumbest thing he'd ever heard of, took the thermos down to the bank in Kyle, and traded all those pre-1900 silver dollars into real money.

## Graduation and War

I'm not saying if you didn't want to go to college after high-school in 1950, you were dumb. But, I will say that luck and timing were against those that didn't, because this country was thrust into war with Korea that fall and anyone outside of college had their butts drafted and most were shipped to the war zone just in time to be shot at by the Red Chinese.

Brothers, Darrell and Darden Ridgeway were a class or two behind David and me, neither signed up for college, one was killed and the other shot up pretty good in the Chinese break-through. Just goes to show you that no matter how small the town or school, when general war starts, everyone and every village is affected.

## Off to College

David LaVern opted for Texas A&M and I decided on Sul Ross State Teachers College in Alpine. We went on our way and seldom saw each other during our college years. After graduation, David LaVern went into the Army for two years and I went into the Air Force for three.

When I was going through flying school in Bartow, Florida, David was stationed at an Army base in north Florida and we did get a visit one time up there. After he got out of the Army, he got a ranch managers job on a fabulous 40,000-acre ranch at Marathon, Texas called the Iron Mountain Ranch. It belonged to the West Foundation out of Houston. When I got out of the Air Force a year later, I went down to our 90,000-acre ranch in Mexico that Dad and his partner from Florida, had bought in 1956.

David and I were in contact with one another and he invited me up to the Marathon ranch for a visit. So, I hopped in our plane, flew up there and landed on the dirt road running up to the headquarters. We spent the next four or five days shooting jackrabbits with our six-shooters out of his jeep. David is one hell of a shot with both six gun and rifle.

I moved back to the Kyle ranch in 1960 and David moved back to his home place on the Blanco River a year or so later.

Last year, we celebrated our 61st Kyle High School Reunion together. He is down at his home place on the Blanco River; going strong, judging Llamas all over the country; and still tough as a pine knot.

AND, he is still the One Most Likely to Succeed and I am probably the One Most Likely To...?

Nothing wrong with all that.

David and his animals

L. D. Bunton

## ANTIOCH COLONY

ANTIOCH COLONY WAS A RURAL FARMING COMMUNITY FORMED DURING RECONSTRUCTION BY A GROUP OF FORMERLY ENSLAVED AFRICAN AMERICANS. ALTHOUGH FREED FROM SLAVERY AFTER THE CIVIL WAR, AFRICAN AMERICANS STILL FOUND IT DIFFICULT TO PURCHASE LAND. IN 1859 ANGLO BUSINESSMAN JOSEPH F. ROWLEY PURCHASED 490 ACRES IN NORTH HAYS COUNTY, ALONG ONION CREEK. HE BEGAN SELLING PARCELS TO FORMER SLAVES IN 1870 AT $5.00 PER ACRE. ROWLEY, PERHAPS IN AN EFFORT TO PROTECT THE NEW LANDOWNERS FROM LOSING THEIR PROPERTY, INDICATED IN MANY OF THE DEEDS THAT THE AFRICAN AMERICAN OWNERS COULD NOT SELL THE PROPERTY WITHOUT ROWLEY'S CONSENT. AFTER MOVING TO MISSOURI, ROWLEY RESCINDED THE STIPULATION IN 1893, BUT THE DOCUMENT WAS NOT FILED IN HAYS COUNTY UNTIL 1913.

COMMUNITY RESIDENTS ELIAS AND CLARISA BUNTON DONATED PROPERTY FOR A COMMUNITY SCHOOL AND CHURCH IN 1874, AND THE BUILDING SERVED AS THE SCHOOL UNTIL 1939. THE FOLLOWING YEAR, THE SCHOOL WAS RELOCATED TO BLACK COLONY ROAD AND SERVED ANTIOCH UNTIL STUDENTS WERE INTEGRATED INTO THE BUDA SCHOOL SYSTEM IN 1961. A BAPTIST CHURCH AND A METHODIST CHURCH WERE ORGANIZED IN THE COMMUNITY, AND THERE WAS ALSO AN ACTIVE MASONIC LODGE AND ORDER OF THE EASTERN STAR CHAPTER IN ANTIOCH.

ANTIOCH REMAINED AN ACTIVE FARM COMMUNITY THROUGH THE 1930s AND 1940s. BY THE 1950s, MANY RESIDENTS HAD MOVED AWAY IN SEARCH OF BETTER EMPLOYMENT OPPORTUNITIES AND THE COMMUNITY WAS VIRTUALLY ABANDONDED. BEGINNING IN THE 1970s FORMER RESIDENTS AND THEIR DESCENDANTS BEGAN RETURNING TO ANTIOCH, SOME PURCHASING THE LAND THAT THEIR ANCESTORS HAD PREVIOUSLY OWNED, AND THE COMMUNITY CONTINUES TO GROW.

(2009)

MARKER IS PROPERTY OF THE STATE OF TEXAS

# L. D. Bunton

## Buda, Texas
## 1900–1983

"Mister Bill,"

"Yes, L. D.,"

"Is you ever had a'nuff nookie?" holding his hand up to his mouth as he always did when he was chuckling. I had no idea what he was talking about, but, Dad sure did. He turned his head toward the window of the pickup so I wouldn't see his smirk and said; "Why do you ask?" knowing full well L. D. knew all about his escapades. Hell, I found out later in life that Dad could have written his Doctorial Thesis on the subject, that is, if he had known how to write.

"Well," said L. D., "if you ever has, then it got to be the nuffius nuff thing you done ever had" and with that both men started laughing.

L. D. was born in the Black colony which is located just west of Buda about 1900 and they both were about the same age. He had been a part of my family's lives since the day he was born.

His father, Pete Bunton, was a bronc breaker for our family on the 101 Ranch west of Buda for years. Tradition has it that Pete would lead a bronc down from the big corrals at the headquarters into a field that was freshly plowed, get on him; and buck him out in the deep fresh dirt of the field. One, if he got bucked off, it wouldn't hurt as bad, and two, a horse can't buck very well in deep dirt.

L. D. had no education, least not that I know of, but he could literally do anything. He could help Dad work cattle horse-back; he could work them in the pens; he could put on a white jacket and completely be at home at any function Dad and Mother might be having. He always had a smile on his face and he was completely unflappable.

But he did have one little habit that would drive Dad crazy. Every fall he would up and quit without notice and leave Dad in a hissie-fit. It didn't matter what he and Dad had planned to do or what ranch work was scheduled, come fall and a whistle from one of his friends over in the Colony and his black you-know-what was gone. Gone cotton picking!

I think he was just recovering from one such venture of "cotton pickin' and girlin," as he called it, when he asked dad that pertinent question.

I ran up on L. D. one day when I went into Buda on business. I walked right up to him, his snow-white hair shining from very old age, and spoke to him softly. He slowly looked up at me, smiled that smile I can remember forever and said; "Mashel, you look mo like yo daddy ever day."

Not long there after, Mother and I went to his funeral. We were the only white folks there. Everyone came up to speak to us and they were so happy we could attend. One niece told Mother that the last time she visited L. D. in the nursing home before he died, he was reminiscing about all his wonderful days on the Kuykendall ranch.

L. D. Bunton was one of those wonderful experiences that very few of us are lucky enough to have in our lives. My life would not be complete without him and the memory it holds.

L. D. Bunton gravestone

I didn't attend the funeral, but I sent a nice letter saying I approved of it.

—Mark Twain

Audie L. Murphy

# Audie L. Murphy

## 1924–1971

Some time in the summer of 1950, General Paul Wakefield, who was with the Texas National Guard at Camp Mabry in Austin, called Dad and invited him to his farm at Monkeyville to meet Audie Murphy. Monkeyville is what the locals called the gasoline service station that was at the intersection on old Hwy 81, where the road turned off to go into Buda. General Wakefield's farm was just over on the east side of the highway from there. Dad whistled me up and I got to ride with him.

Audie Murphy was the most decorated American soldier in WWII. This country had just gone to war with Korea and Audie wanted to join the 36th Division of the Texas National Guard and be in that Texas unit when it went overseas. He had contacted General Wakefield to help him in his endeavor and that is why he was the General's guest over near Buda.

Dad and I drove to the farm and met the General in the yard. He escorted us inside his home and as we did, this rather small, very baby-faced young man walked up and introduced himself to my father. It was Audie Murphy. He was eight years older than I was, but he seemed much younger. I was taken aback by his youthful appearance because I knew who he was by reputation and figured he would be this big, rough and tumble looking fellow, who probably looked like John Wayne.

It just goes to show you, that heroes come in all sizes and the biggest hero of WWII was someone you would never be able to type cast. A simple east Texas farm boy, one of 12 children, who was thrust into the Great War; he fought in eight major campaigns in Sicily, Italy, France and Germany. He participated in two amphibious assaults in Sicily and southern France and was wounded three times.

He received every medal that the United States of America gave for valor; two of them twice. On January 26th, 1945, he was awarded the Medal of Honor for exceptional valor near Holtzwhir, France, where he was personally credited with killing or wounding fifty Germans and stopping an attack by enemy tanks.

He went on to become famous as an actor, and then in May of 1971, he was killed in an airplane crash near Christianburg, Virginia. He was only 47 years old.

He was buried a month later with full military honors near the Tomb of the Unknown Soldier at Arlington National Cemetery in Virginia.

I am honored to be able to say that I met him back in another life time.

Captain Frank A. Hamer

# Captain Frank A. Hamer

## Texas Ranger
## 1884–1955

Captain Frank Hamer was famous for having killed Bonnie Parker and Clyde Barrow back in the early 30s. What a lot of folks don't know was that he was a horseback Ranger back in 1906 and the first man he ever killed was the outlaw Ed Putnam down in Del Rio right after he joined up.

He was sitting on our porch at the ranch one day telling us about it. Seems Putnam got drunk and was shooting up the town when he and some Rangers showed up. Putnam got holed up in a house and started shooting at the Rangers through the windows on either side of the front door. Captain Frank noticed that Ed would shoot

**Clyde Barrow and Bonnie Parker**

through one front window, and then about thirty seconds later, he would shoot at them from the other front window, and so on. Captain Frank immediately noticed there was a definite pattern to his shots. He let this happen about three times, all the while counting the seconds, when it occurred to him that as Ed moved from one side of the front door to the other, he was peeking at them through the key-hole in the front door. As soon as Ed shot the very next time, Captain Frank counted off fifteen seconds and shot through the key-hole of the front door, hitting Brother Ed just underneath his right eye and killed the son of a bitch dead as a hammer.

Dad invited him out to our ranch a lot to hunt or just to sit on the porch so they could visit. I, in the mean time, was down in my room busily reading about Frank and Jesse James, John Wesley Hardin and other famous gun fighters while one of the most famous Texas gunfighters who just about ever lived sat up in our living room. Go figure!

On one of his visits, he started reminiscing about the first time he got shot by a man named McSwain up in Mason County, who obviously had taken a dislike to him. Seems the old man shot him with a shotgun and had it not been for Frank's brother, Harrison, who drug him off and hid him in some brush, McSwain would have found him and finished the job.

Frank's wounds were slow to heal and in an effort to get away from McSwain, he saddled up his pony, loaded up a packhorse and rode SW of Mason until he hit the Pecos River just above its mouth with the Rio Grande, not far from Langtry, Texas. There he set up camp.

He told us he sat on the edge of the high bluff overlooking the Pecos River each morning letting the rays of the sun warm him trying to heal up. During this period of convalescence, he said his favorite spot to sit was in a big mound of interesting pebbles because he could sit there and pitch the pebbles off the high bluff and watch as they hit the water far below.

## The Discovery

He did this day after day as his wounds healed until he had dug himself down in the mound about waist deep. It was then he began to find some bones and realized he had been sitting on top of an ancient grave. He began to pull some of the bones out and he said it was the grave of a giant whose shin bone came up almost to his hip and the skull was twice the size of a normal human being. Not knowing the importance of his find, he pitched them over the bluff into the Pecos River.

After his wounds had completely healed, he headed back home to Mason County and on the way in, stopped by McSwain's ranch house and called him out. The old man hollered out that he thought he had finished him off. Frank hollered back, "No, you didn't, you son of a bitch" and with that both men drew their guns and fired. McSwain missed and Frank Hamer didn't.

He didn't wear cowboy attire like many of the Rangers and in later years always dressed in a suit and tie. He carried a 45 Colt six-shooter in his waistband with the loading gate unlatched so it wouldn't slip down in his pants. I asked him to show it to me one time. It was an engraved six-shooter with a short barrel that he called "Ole Lucky."

Dad said he was a fearless man who had the habit of walking up to an outlaw and slapping the shit out of him and saying; "I'm Frank Hamer." Things kinda came unraveled after that.

When he died, he still carried most of the buckshot in his back from Mr. Mc-Swain's shotgun blast from those days long past. Also, some ten or twelve bullets still remained in his body from several other outlaws as meaningful reminders of countless gunfights over his long Ranger career.

His family asked Dad to be a pallbearer. I had the funeral notice stuck in the "I'm Frank Hamer" presentation book his family gave us. When Dad died in 1976, I went into the library at our ranch to retrieve it and everything was gone.

Everything that is, but this memory.

Clyde and Bonnie's car after shootout

Brigadier General Clarence T. "Curly" Edwinson

# Brigadier General
# Clarence T. "Curly" Edwinson
## 1912–1985

**W**hen I graduated from Kyle high school in 1950, I wanted to attend the best college in Texas that taught Range Management. So, I chose Sul Ross State College in Alpine. No sooner had I arrived in Alpine, Texas that fall of 1950, when the Korean War started. All draft age college men were required to be in a ROTC outfit of some sort in readiness for their required military service and if we weren't, we were subject to immediate induction into the military. Sul Ross had no ROTC attachment to any of the services.

I checked around and several Lone Star Conference colleges (which Sul Ross was a member) did indeed have ROTC units and South West Texas State in San Marcos was one of them that had an Air ROTC Unit. Therefore, I was obliged to transfer to San Marcos after only one semester at Sul Ross, which happened to be only 20 miles from our ranch. It was not my wish to be that close but fate chose otherwise. Nor did I have any desire to be in the Air Force after graduation but funny things happen when one is not paying attention.

My so-called prior military experience was one and a half years at San Marcos Baptist Academy back in my grade school years but one thing I do remember about that sorry place, is we learned how to march "in step" and carry a 1903 bolt action Springfield rifle. So, since ROTC is part classroom studies and a bunch of marching in ranks, I had noted this prior military experience on my résumé and was therefore immediately made commander of the Color Guard. The Color Guard is a group of four individuals who carry the American flag and others in all the parades, etc. So, for the first three years at SWT, that was my military job. My fourth or senior year, I was commander of one the four squadrons. The Air Force calls them squadrons; the Infantry calls them Companies.

But, digressing just for a minute, all college and university ROTC individuals are required to attend a four week ROTC training course between their Junior and Senior years. In can be any where in the United States. Ours happened to be in Riverside, California in the summer of 1953. Most of the universities and colleges of Texas attended that one. There were a ton of students. Texas A&M and many other schools were represented.

The military bunch in the AF-ROTC processing area took one look at me in my Stetson cowboy hat and immediately singled me out for a publicity shot which appeared in the local Riverside newspaper. I think they had me riding a jackass carrying a golf bag or some such nonsense.

**MEK entering Riverside ROTC**

## ROTC SUMMER CAMP-RIVERSIDE, CALIFORNIA
## JULY 1953

Again, my fancy résumé came into play and I was immediately made commander of the Color Guard for the entire camp which had a military marching review each of the four Saturdays we were there. When one is marching with the Color Guard, one is not allowed to "retreat" the American flag (backup), therefore one must always move forward or swing the foursome in either a left or right oblique movement when one wants to alter or reverse course. I figured out a fun move where we would front-step, side step the flags so we could reverse our position when we needed to do so. On the third weekend as I approached the reviewing stand where all the Officers and dignitaries were located, I heard the Commanding General tell one of his guests, "Watch the Color Guard, they do an interesting maneuver," which we did. Because of my work commanding the "Colors," I was asked to be the Commander of the whole camp for our fourth and final week of the camp.

When it was all said and done, I was awarded a trophy as "Outstanding Cadet" for the third week. I add this in all modesty, the trophies were engraved between the third and fourth week of our stay. After my performance as Commander of the whole camp for our graduation ceremonies, the Air Force officer in charge of my group, pulled me off to one side and said he was sorry to inform me that had they been able to vote over again, that I would have been awarded the "Outstanding Cadet" of the whole camp, not just the third week trophy. He said the trophies had to be engraved in advance. Kinda wish he hadn't told me.

**MEK Outstanding Cadet 3rd Week**

**MEK Cadet Commander 4th Week**

## Graduation and Entry into the US Air Force
## Flight Schools and Pilot Training

Well, any-hoo, cutting to the chase. I graduated from SWT and was mustered into the US Air Force at Lackland AFB in San Antonio in the summer of 1954 and was immediately transferred to Bartow AFB in central Florida to begin my training as an air force pilot. During that six month period I learned how not to crash an AT-6 single engine airplane and upon graduation from that school, I was transferred to Goodfellow AFB in San Angelo, Texas where I learned the same thing about a B-25 twin engine WWII medium bomber. (Class of 55-T) From there, I was transferred to Lockbourne AFB in Columbus, Ohio. I was supposed to be in a KC-97 Tanker re-fueling squadron but it just so happened that when I arrived, my unit was TDY (temporary duty) to England so my skinny butt was transferred into a B-47 squadron the next day.

The military does not care one bit what your qualifications are. If you have warm blood in your body, they will find a slot somewhere and that's where you will end up. That's when I figured out that the military can drive a square peg into a round hole no matter what. It's simply the size of the hammer driving the peg.

## The General

Well, while I was rattling around in the B-47 squadron, which was training 24 hours a day how to fly over the north pole and bomb the shit out of Russia, my father was drinking some really smooth whiskey with everyone at the Austin Country Club, which just so happened to include the Commander of Bergstrom AFB, a feller by the name of Gen. Clarence T. Edwinson, better known to all the drinkers simply as "Curly." Well, let me tell you, he was a booger. But that is another story.

After several rounds of some good whiskey, one of the patrons of the Country Club asked the good General why in the hell he didn't have Bill Kuykendall's son, an outstanding Air Force officer, working for him at Bergstrom and the General took another big gulp of whiskey and said "By God, I'll take care of that!"

About a week later, I am just coming in from ferrying a bunch of Colonels over to Salina, Kansas in one of the two B-25s at Lockbourne AFB, and when I walked in to Base Ops, an officer there tells me the Commanding General of the base wants me to call him immediately. I do not have a clue what is going on so I dial the number I was given and the General's Aide answers and says; "General Wheelus wants to talk to you." Turns out General Wheelus was an old Texas boy from Menard, Texas. He gets on the line and tells me he has had a call from the Commander of Bergstrom AFB in Austin, Texas, one General Edwinson, who wants me to work for him and for me to pack my bags and head for Texas.

## G T T
## (Gone To Texas)

I answered "Yes, sir" and a few days later I was packed and headed for Texas.

## Arrival at Bergstrom AFB

As soon as I arrived in Austin, I checked in at Bergstrom AFB to meet my new boss, General Edwinson. The General did not office in the main headquarters building at Bergstrom; his office was in the Base Ops building down on the flight line. It was one big, square room and when you opened the door and stepped in, the General's desk was catty-cornered across the room from the door; his aide de camp, Captain Harry Russell, sat immediately to the left, over in one corner, and Mildred, his secretary; sat directly in front of the door, over in the other corner. It was a bit bazaar.

Anyway, I knocked and stepped into the room and reported to the General. He stood and shook my hand, welcomed me to Austin and nodded at Captain Russell and said, "He will tell you what to do." And that was the start of quite a year for me in the US Air Force. I guess I was being groomed to be the future aide de camp to the General after Captain Russell left, but for the remaining year that I was in the Air Force, (July 1965-July 1957) I was his "Lemon-aide." Translated to mean; I carried his flight bag on to his air plane and stirred his drinks when they needed stirring, which was often. I probably should have paid the Air Force for my last year of service instead of the other way round.

## An Amazing Experience

I was soon to find out that I was serving under a very famous military man who had fought through WWII as a P38 pilot; had flown every airplane known to man; had made full bird Colonel at the age of 29; was General Curtis E. LeMay's ex-brother-in-law; had served under LeMay in many military situations; was one hell of a warrior; one hell of a brawler and probably didn't know what to do with himself during peace time.

He was the epitome, or fit the mold of the General, in General Patton's statement "that all great war time Generals should probably be killed by the last bullet of the last battle' because they become misfits in peace time." I am not saying General Ed was a misfit. He wasn't. But, he had been a great warrior in WWII and peace-time was unsettling for him, I'm sure.

## His Story

Brig. General Clarence Theodore Edwinson was born in Kansas on July 1st, 1912. He was a highly decorated WWII fighter pilot, collegiate football star and world champion skeet shooter.

At Washburn University he was a four year letterman in football and in 1932 was named to the All Central Conference team as running back and was honorable mention for the AP All American team. He had also lettered in basketball in 1929. The 1933 Washburn yearbook described him as probably the greatest halfback ever to play for Washburn University. Washburn coach, Ernest Bearg, said that Edwinson was one of the best backs in all football, that in his 17 years of coaching only Red Grange of Illinois and Glen Presnell of Nebraska were his equals. In 1970, Washburn University inducted him into its Athletics Hall of Fame.

He enlisted into the Army Air Corp as a flying cadet in 1934. Then, he advanced in rank and became a second lieutenant in 1936. The following year until 1940, he served as an instructor and flight commander at Randolph Field in San Antonio, Texas. That same year (1940) he was sent to England as a military observer with the Fighter Command of the Royal Air Force during the battle of Britain. (He told me that while there he flew several times in a RAF Spitfire) He returned to the States in March of 1942.

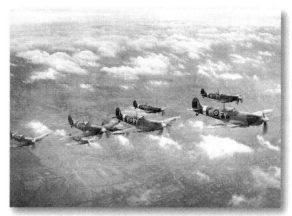

**Spitfires in The Battle of Britain**

## WWII

General Ed assumed several commands of different fighter squadrons' state-side and then in August 1944, he was designated commander of the 82$^{nd}$ Fighter Group of P-38s stationed in Italy.

## The Incident

Edwinson was in command there when a controversial incident took place in November of that year when American pilots shot down four Soviet Yaks. Here is the story described in *Combat Aircraft of WWII* by Glenn B. Bavousett:

> "The first engagement occurred in early November 1944, over Yugoslavia. Russian ground forces had the Germans in retreat. The 15th Air Force was requested to provide close air support. Colonel C. T. "Curly" Edwinson's 82nd Fighter Group operating from Foggia, Italy, caught the mission. The Husky P-38's performance was so good that the Russians asked for a repeat support mission to be flown by the same group the following day. Again, Edwinson led his three squadrons of P-38s across the Adriatic and down the valleys of mountainous Yugoslavia. Unknown to Edwinson a crisis was in the

making. The Russians failed to advise Foggia that during the interval between the previous day's support mission and now, Russian ground forces had advanced the battle line by 100 kilometers. Edwinson led the P-38s into the strafing attack that ripped first into the Germans then immediately into the Russians. The resulting devastation was both massive and effective. Caught in the strafing was a Russian staff car. Its occupant, a three star general (Lt. Gen. G. P. Kotov, commander of XI Guards Rifle Corps) was killed, a victim of lack of communications and close similarity between German and Russian Uniforms and vehicle color schemes. And with the P-38's speed these differences went unnoticed. A flight of Yaks were in the vicinity and the call went out for them to attack the P-38s still busy making strafing runs. Caught totally by surprise, Edwinson saw two of his aircraft being shot down. Instantly, he signaled the squadron to disengage from ground attack and fight their way out of the valley. During a brief air battle that ensued Edwinson's P-38 pilots knocked down four of the Yaks and sent the remainder scurrying away into the haze. One of the four Yaks that really got it was the unlucky fellow whose course took him directly over the guns of a P-38 piloted by Bill Blurock who was in a stall condition and but a few yards under the Russian. A touch of the button and the Yak was literally ripped to shreds. This incident over Yugoslavia gave the United States a 4 to 2 edge in the only known aerial combat between the two powers. When advised that the situation was one of those unfortunate happenings that bad communications sometimes foster, and after all, it was the Russians who attacked the P-38's, the Russians promptly shot all those involved on their end and demanded the same be done to Edwinson, the leader of the P-38's. "Curly" Edwinson was quietly and hastily re-assigned to a base out of Europe."

The General told me in 1956 that he still had the combat film from that raid and when the next war started between the US and Russia, that he would be proud to say he had killed the first Russian son of a bitch. I never had a chance to see the film.

By the end of the war he had flown 30 combat missions and logged several thousand hours of flight time.

In May of 1946, during the height of the Berlin airlift, he assumed command of the 366th Fighter Group stationed at Fritzlar, Air Base, Germany. Then became commander of the 27th Fighter Group; then commanded the 86th Composite Group at Bad Kissengen Air Base, Germany. At the time the 86th was the only combat-capable fighter group of the USAF in Europe. General Curtis LeMay regarded Edwinson as his

Lockheed P-38 Lightning

best combat commander during this period. LeMay planned to use Edwinson's P-47s (changed airplanes) if he needed to take offensive actions against the Russians to keep Berlin supplied.

General Curtis E. LeMay

Edwinson returned to the United States in June of 1949 and continued to work for General LeMay in SAC (Strategic Air Command) in different commands. On April 6th, 1951, he assumed command of the 42nd Air Division, SAC, at Bergstrom Air Force Base, in Austin, Texas. While there, he was promoted to Brig. General on December 15th, 1953. He continued to be the commander there until the late summer of 1957.

He retired from active service in 1961 and moved back to Austin, Texas. He died in June of 1985 while living across the street on Stratford Drive from Dr. Bob Morrison, one of my oldest friends. Captain, now Colonel Harry Russell, also retired in Austin, called me and I attended his funeral. He was buried with full military honors in Ft. Sam Houston National Cemetery in San Antonio, Texas.

Some of Brig. General Clarence T. (Curly) Edwinson's decorations include: The Distinguished Flying Cross; the Air Medal with three oak leaf clusters; and the French Croix de Guerre with Palm.

## Back to My Year at Bergstrom AFB

I had barely unpacked my bags when Capt. Russell informed me that one of the many duties we had to perform each week was play basketball and I was nearly fired before the ink had dried on my transfer. Seems that the good General liked to play half court basketball and his team was called the "Bone Crushers." Me, being the newest member of the group, I got to play defense with the opposition.

## The Bone Crushers

I was a pretty decent basketball player so I looked forward to the scrimmage. Well, let me tell you, the General was a very big man and one hell on an athlete. He could do anything with a basketball. We hadn't been in the game more than 10 minutes when someone passed the ball to the General and he broke for the basket, knocked me aside and made an easy lay-up. I jumped back in the way and probably snarled something like "Just try that again, buster," whereby the General nodded at one of his team mates and they pitched him the ball and he broke for the basket again. This time he ran right over the top of me, slapped the shit out of me as he passed, knocking me to the floor and made another easy lay-up, but this time with the other hand.

**The Bone Crushers**

Well, I jumped up from the floor to say I don't know what, when Captain Russell, who played on the General's side, saved my skinny white ass. He stepped right up close and blocked me from doing anything and as he did he whispered in a very low voice; "Learn to take it or you are fired." I had sense enough, thank God, to take a deep breath, smile, nod, and get back in the game. Two weeks later, Russell said I could play on their side which I did for the rest of the year. The General had his own ways of testing everyone. It was what it was. I'll relate others in a moment.

A few weeks after this incident, Russell told me that just before I had shown up, that some professional basketball team had requested permission to work out in the AF Base gym there. They just happened to be practicing one day when the General showed up and asked if they wanted to play a half court ball. Everyone agreed, of course, and Russell said within 5 minutes the General had either run over or knocked down just about every one of them and they stormed off of the court never to return. Russell laughed and said it was one of their better games.

Russell told me that when the good Colonel (later General) first took over command at Bergstrom (before Russell became his aide de camp) that he had gotten rip-roaring drunk down at the Officers Club one night, climbed up on the bar, told everyone in no uncertain terms he was their new commander and that he could whip any son of a bitch on the base. Well, it turns out there was a big Lieutenant who was just about as tough as Edwinson and in the ensuing scuffle, he knocked the Colonel on his ass before cooler heads prevailed and were able to stop the fight.

The following morning, Colonel Edwinson invited the young Lieutenant into his office, told him very quietly that it was obvious that Bergstrom AFB was too small for the both of them and where would the Lieutenant like to be transferred. And that was that; shades of John Wayne.

## To Fish or Not to Fish
## Therein Lies the Question

In 1956, Bergstrom AFB controlled or owned Matagorda Island which had a paved runway. The General was a big fisherman, so every week or so he would announce that all were going to fish and the first weekend he did, I had a date with a good looking blonde in Austin. He walked by me and said, "Kirk, you want to go fishing?" I said, "General, I've got a hot date with this good looking blonde tonight, can I go next time?" Well, he went fishing three more times and left my butt on the base. About the 4th time he said- "You want to go fishing?" I answered, "Yes sir, got my bag packed right here in the hall closet." He grinned and said, "Well, get your ass on my airplane."

## The Airplane

The General's airplane was an old B-26 salvaged from WWII. I had several hundred hours of time in a B-25 but, I'm here to tell you, the only similarity between the two was both had twin engines. Both were tricycle geared, twin engine medium WWII bombers. But, that is where the similarity stopped! The B-25 was a stable airplane that had a crew of some 5 or 6 men during the war, whereas the B-26 was more of a twin engine fighter, with room for only the pilot and maybe a tail gunner. The pilot and co-pilot entered the B-25 from under the belly where the pilot of the B-26 crawled up the side of the airplane and stepped into the cockpit from the open canopy, just like a fighter. The B-25 had a hydraulic breaking system that was very easy to work and one could put the brakes in place, and easily run up the 1200 horse engines on the airplane and do all the pre-flight checks necessary. The B-26, however, had little bitty rudder (brake) pedals, and two 2600 horse engines that when I ran the airplane up, I had to stand up on the breaks just to keep the damn thing from creeping. That airplane was hot as a firecracker and I'm sure that is why the General loved it. He never offered to let me fly it and I was glad that he didn't. I didn't like that airplane.

**WWII B-26 Marauder**

## Some Flying Experiences with the General

Here are a couple of incidents I had while flying with him: We were down at Matagorda on one fishing trip and he wanted to fly out into the gulf and see if we could find any schools of red fish. So, he cranked up the airship and we took off in a big circle to see what we could find. Now, the B-25 cruises at about 160 mph where the B-26 cruises way over that. Now, as mentioned, the B-26 does not have a co-pilot seat, just a jump seat on the right side. So, the General strapped himself in the pilot seat, cigar firmly clenched in his teeth, and you know-who strapped "hisself" into the jump-seat provided and off to the rodeo we went.

We hadn't been out over 30 minutes or so when the General became a bit bored and looked over at me and said, "Watch this Lieutenant," trying all the while to have a big grin on his face and hold on to his cigar at the same time. With that, he dropped the airplane right down on top of the water and kicked "er" up a notch until we were running close to 250 mph. He got so close to the water that the props were kicking up some spray, then to make things more interesting, he rolled the airplane ever so slightly to the left until the wingtip started picking up some spray also. Then, just for fun, he rolled it over to the right and did the same thing on that side. All the time looking at me and grinning that shit-eating grin that a kid gets on their face when they are really having fun. I was so scared that I was numb. I just looked straight ahead and held on to my jump-seat so tightly that my knuckles turned white. He had a strange way of testing his hired help. I don't hold it against him. If war started tomorrow and we all had to fight, he would be my first choice as my commander. But, he could be one crazy son of a bitch if the need arose. And, let me tell you friend, there are times in war when there "ain't nothing bad" about that!

This one is funny: Another time we were down at Matagorda and were loaded up to come back to Bergstrom, when a damn F-80 Shooting Star two place jet fighter was granted access to the runway in front of the General. Well, that pissed him off and he called the little control tower and told them he wanted to be first. They answered and told him ever so politely that he was "number two" for takeoff, not number one. Well, that was the second time he said; "Watch this Lieutenant" and I damn near shit, cause he taxied out on to the active runway without permission from the tower, and rolled right up behind the jet, so close the nose of the B-26 was in the exhaust of the F-80. I braced myself cause I thought he was gonna jam the nose of our airplane up their ass, he was so close, in fact, the man in the rear seat turned ever so slightly and all he could see were two of the biggest propellers turning over he had ever seen in his life. His damn eyes got as big a sauce pans.

## The Race to Bergstrom

The pilot of the jet did his run-up, so the General did his. Then the General looked over at me with a big grin and said; "That son of a bitch is going to 20,000 feet and we are going to 200 feet and we will beat his ass back to Bergstrom." About that time the pilot of the jet released his brakes for his take-off roll, so, shit, we released ours. One must remember that on a take-off roll, a B-26 can out accelerate a jet, so the General had to be careful that we wouldn't whack him going down the runway. About that time, the pilot of the jet eased it off the runway, so the General followed suit and jerked our plane off of the runway at the same time. The jet pulled straight up to go to 20,000 feet and we turned left to go to 200 feet and the race was on. I don't think the General ever retarded the throttles and by the time we crossed the channel headed inland. We were smoking!

We hadn't gone 20 miles inland when the General spotted some ole rice farmer tooling along in his pickup at right angles to our flight path. He eased the nose over just a smidgen until we were right in the dirt and we roared past the front bumper of that old man at about 300 plus miles per hour and when I looked back over my shoulder, the farmer had run his pickup out into the rice field. I loved it. AND, we had to climb to get over Pilot Knob right near Bergstrom. In the mean time, we were taxing up to shut down the airplane when the jet landed. We beat his ass back to Bergstrom.

## The Rules

The military can be real chicken shits and they obviously want you to follow the rules. I never was a very good rule follower then and neither am I now. The General wasn't either and I think that's why I liked him so much. He didn't give a damn about anything. Bergstrom was his base and by God he could run it anyway he wanted, so long as he landed his airplane on the numbers.

I have never read the 40 biographies on General LeMay and don't intend to do so now, but it has always been my opinion that no one in the Air Force dared touch General Ed as long as LeMay ran SAC out of Omaha. I think Bergstrom was the only fighter base in the country still controlled by SAC. One does not get promoted in the military for being a brawler and a fist fighter and one certainly does not get promoted if one throws a full bird colonel through the plate glass window of the officers club at Bergstrom, which I heard General Ed did a couple of years before I got there. But I sincerely believe that LeMay liked and understood who General Ed was. When LeMay needed his help during the war and afterwards during the Berlin air lift, he always knew that if he was going to get into one hell of a fist fight with the Russians or anyone else, he could always rely on Edwinson to lead the fight. Whether he did anything or not to protect General Ed at Bergstrom I shall leave up to the historians to ferret out. I only feel like if Gen. LeMay needed any rough job done that he could pick up his "Red Phone" in Omaha and dial General Ed's number and it would get done. And, on top of everything, I think LeMay really liked his old ex-brother-in-law war horse, warts and all. Besides all that, General LeMay liked to fish.

However, I don't think many other General officers in SAC felt the same way. A case in point: By the time I was at Bergstrom the General had quit flying the F-84 (Lead Sleds-as they were called), but he had been flying them a few years earlier.

## The Non-accident

One day he was leading a flight of four F-84s on a practice mission and it became apparent that they needed to be re-fueled. The closest SAC base to their flight was Carswell AFB in Ft. Worth so the General signaled his group that they would land there. Turns out there was a heavy rain squall in the area and when they hit the runway they immediately started hydroplaning and had no breaking action what-so-ever. With no hesitation at all, General Ed said "Two to the left" and "Two to the right," and out into the deep mud they plowed. All the aircraft came to a stop in the wet dirt with no damage, other than shit slung everywhere. The Carswell AFB maintenance folks ran out with a couple of cranes and cables, pulled them out of the mud, washed them down in no time and they were as good as new.

In the mean time, as the planes were getting retrieved and cleaned up, General Ed got a call that the two star General in command of Carswell wanted his ass in his office pronto. So, Gen Ed in flight suit and all, went up to the man's office and reported in, only to have his ass chewed out for running his airplanes off in the mud and the commanding General said he was going to write him up for the "accident" he caused.

General Ed, still standing at attention, let him finish and then he said: "General, there WAS no accident. By running off into the mud, I saved all four of MY airplanes and now I am going out on the flight line and take MY airplanes back to MY base at Bergstrom. Is there anything else you need from me?" And with that, he saluted, turned on his heel and left. OR, fuck you and the horse you rode in on!

## The Fire

Whenever we were going to Matagorda it was my job to have the General's shit all loaded on the B-26 and to take it out run it up and warm up the engines. So, one day the crew chief and I got everything ship shape, got aboard, cranked that big sucker up and taxied out to the run-up area. On the way out I noticed a flick on the gas gauge on the left engine and mentioned it to the sergeant. I locked up the brakes as best I could and brought the big engines up to "run-up power" and as I did, I noticed that the gas gauge flicked one more time and just as I turned to say something to the chief, the left engine blew up and caught on fire. I immediately advanced the throttles on both engines to almost take-off power to see if I could blow out the flames and when I did the flame from that engine blew almost all the way back to the tail section, it was that bad. I then chopped all the power on both engines and called the tower.

Now, everyone on the base knew that 136 was the General's airplane and when I broke through to the tower and said, "Tower, this is 136, I have an emergency, my left engine is on fire," all hell broke loose in the tower. I could see the little figures up there nearly running into one another like a bunch of Keystone Cops, all hollering that that damn dumb shit of a lieutenant is burning up the fucking General's airplane. In two seconds you have never seen so many fire-trucks busting out on the flight tarmac in your life; must have been 10 of them.

There was no internal fire-extinguisher system in the B-26, nothing. So, Sergeant what's-his-face crew-chief, grabs a little tiny fire-extinguisher we had in the cockpit, jumps out the front trap door of the airplane and runs up and squirts it into the open front face of the left engine. All it did was make the flames turn a bright orange color and with that he takes off in a dead run to get away from the airplane and at about 50 yards, he whirls around and looking at me, starts making the slashing motion across his throat. *NO SHIT!*

I had chopped the throttles by this time and the left engine has stopped burning back past the wing but is back firing, which makes the prop spin like the old wheel on a Fair-banks/Morse single cylinder engine. And with that, I bailed out over the side, barely missing the back-firing prop, and take off down the tarmac myself as the biggest fire-truck you have ever seen comes sliding right up to the airplane. It had one of those enormous fire-extinguisher guns mounted on the roof and two side mounts that were hand held. Since the fire was not as evident as before, this little bitty airman jumps out of the fire truck, runs to the side and grabs one of the side mounted hoses and runs up with it and stands on his tip-toes and peers into the front cowl of the engine and just as he did, the damn engine back-fired again, blowing his hat off. The little devil cut loose with that fire hose full of foam, completely missing the engine in question, but squirting directly into the open cockpit completely fucking up the General's uniform I had hung in there.

Any time there was an emergency on base, our office phone would ring, telling the General, et al, what the problem was. Well, obviously that had happened, because at that very moment a staff car came sliding up beside me and the staff driver said: "Get in Lieutenant," and I did. We roared back to Base Ops and I stepped out, went through the corridor and opened the door to our mutual office just as the General was walking across the room to see what was going on. I snapped to attention, saluted and said: "General, I just tried to burn up your airplane." He looked at me and answered: "Kirk," he very seldom called me that, "Are you alright?" I said, "Yes sir." He then said, "Go sit down, I will take care of it." And he did. I never heard another word about the incident other than the report the crew chief gave him several days later explaining the cause of the fire.

Had I been in any other outfit in the military, they would have had me in full dress uniform the following day on the tarmac with drum and bugle-corp, playing while the commanding General snipped the buttons off of my clothes just before facing a firing squad, but not General Ed.

About a week later, Dad was in town and we all went down to the Officer's Club for a drink. The General told dad that the gas line between the pressure pump and the engine had ruptured and had we taken off for Matagorda Island that morning with the engines running at full power, the flame would have cut the wing completely off just like a cutting torch. He told Dad we were damn lucky I discovered it on the run-up or we'd all be deader than hell.

And, again, I never saw a report nor was written up for anything. When that General said he'd take care of it, by God he meant it.

## Captain Harry Russell Aide De Camp

I have said very little about Captain Harry Russell, the General's Aide de Camp. Russ was a hoot, but he was also a tiger just like the General. The little fucker was not afraid of man nor beast. He had been a flying sergeant during WWII and had been at Bergstrom in the old days when they were training glider pilots. He being in the gliders. I can remember them well because the C-47s out of Bergstrom would drag two or three of them over the ranch in the early days of the war and fly over our house. Each C-47 would be towing them and this was early training for the D-Day landing. Russell did not make it to the D-Day landing. I can't remember where he was stationed.

Russ was a rare individual and one of the funny habits he had was to tell me a new joke every single day I was around him. I swear, he never told me one twice. People all over the Air Force knew him and would call him on the hot line in our office just to tell him a new one.

He was able to get a job in the Pentagon after working for General Ed and he immediately went to work for the Chief of Staff or someone pretty high up on the US

Air Force food chain, because when he retired in the 1960s, he was a full bird. Not bad for a lowly Captain in 1957.

When he got out of the Air Force, he, too, moved to Austin, Texas and I bumped into him from time to time. He was a booger and I liked the hell out of him.

## 1952 ISSF Shooting Championships
## Oslo, Norway

Not only was General Ed one of the finest halfbacks and basketball stars ever to come out of Washburn University at Topeka, Kansas in the early 30s, he was one of the best shotgun shooters in the world by 1950.

I learned this by accident just like everything else I learned in my short 12 month stint working for him at Bergstrom AFB.

One day, we were tooling around the base in his light blue Cadillac convertible when he turned into the shooting range on the base. I didn't even know there was one. He said, "You want to shoot a little skeet, Lieutenant?" "Yes Sir," I replied.

We walked into the store room where the guns were stored and there in an old rack were 30 Model 12, 12-gauges; all numbered 1-30 on the wrists, and all with Cutts Compensators. The General picked one up, handed me one, grabbed several boxes of shells and we went out on the range for me to witness some of the fanciest shotgun shooting I have ever seen in my life. There was no position, no stance, and no station, where he couldn't hit every single target. I think he could have placed the shotgun over his shoulder and used a mirror like Adolph (Ad) Toepperwein of San Antonio and still hit every one of them. His final stunt was to stand next to the low-box, holler PULL, and shoot that son of a bitch from the hip.

That's when I found out the General had shot a perfect score of 150 out of 150 at the 1952 ISSF World Shooting Championships in Oslo, Norway. It was known at the time as the 35th UIT World Shooting Championships. The event took place just weeks before the 1952 Summer Olympics.

Several months later, it was decided to close the shooting range and sell off all the shotguns. So, we loaded up again and went back over because the General wanted a bunch of them. They were offered to us at $30 bucks a piece and he bought several and I bought just one, ole number 17.

Still have it after all these years; never had a finer shotgun.

## The End of the Road for Everyone

As General Patton said at the end of the movie, "All good things have to come to an end." My mustering out date of July, 1957 came to fruition. The General very cordially offered me a "Captaincy" and a job as his aide de camp if I would stay in the service, but we all knew I wouldn't. The previous fall, Dad and his partner bought an 139 section ranch in the state of Coahuila, Mexico and I was packed and ready to head down there and become another Mexican.

That same July, General Curtis LeMay quit the Strategic Air Command, where he had run the whole US Air Force for years, and moved up to Assistant Chief of Staff US Air Force. The screen door hadn't any more than hit LeMay in the ass until the "Higher Ups" running SAC out of Omaha, Nebraska canned General Ed for all of his past transgressions (which, I'm sure were considered numerous) and shipped his butt to upper Michigan, or as they say in the trade: Put him out to pasture! I supposed one in the Air Force can't get further out in the boonies, than to have to work the Canadian Dew Line, which is what the northern protective radar line was called in those days. I guess it was better than having to work in a damn missile silo 400 feet below the surface of the earth just west of Roswell, NM, but I doubt it.

When we all get to VALHALLA and are turned into young warriors once again, you will find me standing next to General Clarence Theodore Edwinson, because he was one fighting son of a bitch, and I am immensely proud that our lives touched, ever so briefly.

It is generally advisable never to eject directly over the area you have just bombed.

—US AIR FORCE MANUAL

MEK and Ole #17—Blue Quail
Sierra Hermosa Ranch, Mexico 1958

Jim Hairston

# James Walter Hairston

## Rice's Crossing, Texas
## 1916–1988

Jim Hairston was my best buddy and the son of a bitch wouldn't give me my gold-top presentation cane back. So, I figured out a way to get even and here is what I did; I went to about 12 antique shops down on South Congress Avenue in Austin until I found and bought not one cane, but two; one with a silver top and one with a gold top. Then, I had Bill Rider make me a fancy wooded presentation, velvet lined box then I swung by Austin Engraving and had them engrave an inscription on a silver plaque and screwed that sucker to the lid on the box. Which said, and I quote:

TO THE

HONORABLE COMMANDER JAMES WALTER HAIRSTON

V.C., D.S.O., AND TWO BARS. M.V.O., S.S.

OF THE DESTROYER H.M.S. GILMER

WITH AFFECTION FROM

COLONEL MARSHALL EARLY KUYKENDALL

CHIEF OF SCOUTS, HIS MAJESTY'S OWN GUARDS

SCOTTISH HIGHLAND REGIMENT, 79TH FOOT

IN REMEMBRANCE OF OUR MANY CAMPAIGNS TOGETHER

NOVEMBER 25TH, 1916

Then, Betty and I whistled up about 50 of our friends and we all headed out to Oak Hill to the Acapulco Restaurant and Bar for what we called the "Get the Gold Topped Cane back from Jim Hairston party." Just a small side bar; while buying the other canes, I found a wooden walking stick with a round top which I promptly spray painted with gold paint, tied an orange piece of surveying tape on it and had it laying on top of the bar in readiness for the big exchange about to take place.

Just before it became evident that most of us were slightly beyond being able to stand erect, I whistled everyone to be quiet, got Jim to come forward and bring me back my gold topped presentation cane. The cane had been given to my great grandfather in 1888 and made the exchange for the new spray painted gold topped sorry piece of junk for my museum piece. Everyone hooted and hollered their approval, and just as Jim turned to leave, I said, "Hey, wait a minute." Reached under the table and pulled out the presentation box with the two beautiful canes inside and handed it to him. He set it down on the table, read the inscription, then opened it and saw the two canes. Tears started running down his face and he leaned over and softly said, "You Son of a Bitch" and I said, "Yeah, right back at you."

Jim had been my best buddy for years, but he was my really "bestist" buddy when he was my Best Man in my marriage to Betty Lou in 1985. But, I am getting ahead of myself.

## The Naval Academy

Jim was born in 1916 in Bartlett, Texas. His family had inherited a 600 acre black land farm over at Rice's Crossing nearby from his Uncle Jim Kuykendall, a distant relative of ours from the Missouri bunch. Jim went to all the local Williamson County schools and then in 1937 was appointed to the Naval Academy at Annapolis, Maryland by a US Congressman, who was a friend of the family. Prior to his appointment, Jim also attended the University of Texas at Austin studying to be a Civil Engineer.

Jim went there a couple of years when he began developing some sort of eye problems that caused him to need glasses. Turns out in those days, one had to have perfect vision to attend the Academy's and he was washed out. He returned home and worked as a Civil Engineer on the Marshall Ford Dam, Texas and the Denison Dam, Texas/Oklahoma project until the Japs decided to bomb Pearl Harbor on Sunday, December the 7th, 1941. Shortly thereafter, every man and boy in Williamson County decided to join the military. Jim enlisted on April 24th of 1942 at a Naval Recruiting office in Durant, Oklahoma as a Seaman.

He wasn't in very long, when he was transferred to of all places, the Aleutian Islands off the coast of Alaska. The Japs had invaded and occupied one or more of the Island chain, and the US military figured they'd better do something about it.

Jim had been there no time at all, when he was asked to report to an officer stationed there for some duty that needed to be performed. Jim walked in, saluted, stated his name and the officer raised his head up from his paper work and exclaimed, "Hairston, what in the hell are you doing here?" Turns out the officer had been a classmate of Jim's at the Naval Academy, Class of 1940 or 41.

Well in no time at all, the officer had Jim a commission as an officer, had him shipped to Florida, where Jim promptly volunteered to be placed in one of the first under-water demolition teams formed in the Second World War. Obviously, Jim loved the water. He told me he was trained to swim in to a beach, attach TNT around the top of a coral reef, set the timer, and swim away before it blew up. As soon as he finished his

**Lt. (jg) James W. Hairston**

training, he boarded the US Destroyer Gilmer and shipped out to the Pacific for the duration of the war.

*(Records state that Jim was an Enlisted Seaman until he was appointed to be an officer on June 1st, of 1943. The Naval Records further note that Lt. (jg) James W. Hairston, who was a member of the Underwater Demolition Team Five, participated in the invasions of Saipan, Tinian, Leyte and Luzon Islands from February 1944 to 1 March 1945. Jim was awarded the Philippine Liberation Ribbon and one bronze star for his participation in the operations on Leyte and joining Islands from 17 October to 20 October, 1944.)*

His ship would steam in close to the Island to be invaded, and dump the team off in the water. Jim, with the TNT wrapped around his waist, his primitive eye goggles on and a knife strapped to his belt, would then swim into the Jap held Island, get up to the coral reefs, dive down attach the TNT to the tops, light the fuse, and swim away. The TNT would blow the tops off of the corral so the Marines in their landing crafts, could pass over the tops of the coral on their way to the beaches.

Jim called the Japs on the beaches, Charley. Said Charley would stand out there all day and shoot at them, but because of the way the Pacific Ocean swells would rise and fall, Charley could never hit them. So, after a while, they paid them no attention and went on about their chores. But, he said on those few occasions when the Japs decided to try and drop some mortars on them, that was a different ball game. The first few times they were hit with mortars, several of the team members were badly hurt, not from shrapnel, but from the horrible concussion that occurred when the blast went off under water. They quickly learned to immediately float on top of the water so the concussion was not so bad. But, as Jim said, it got pretty hairy in a hurry during those times.

THE SECRETARY OF THE NAVY
WASHINGTON

The President of the United States takes pleasure in presenting the SILVER STAR MEDAL to

LIEUTENANT, JUNIOR GRADE, JAMES WALTER HAIRSTON
UNITED STATES NAVAL RESERVE

for service as set forth in the following

CITATION:

"For conspicuous gallantry and intrepidity as Leader of an Underwater Demolition Unit in a daylight reconnaissance of enemy Japanese-held Saipan Island beeches on June 14, 1944. Undaunted by a prolonged and heavy concentration of mortar, machine-gun, and sniper fire which killed or wounded several or his crew, Lieutenant, Junior Grade, (then Ensign) Hairston courageously led his men to a point within 30 yards of the beach and, fearlessly penetrating the dangerous sector, obtained valuable information for the landing force. By his outstanding leadership, perseverance and zealous devotion to duty in the face of grave peril, Lieutenant, Junior Grade, Hairston contributed materially to the success of our operations in this strategic area and upheld the highest traditions of the United States Naval Service."

For the President,

*James Forrestal*

Secretary of the Navy

**Silver Star Citation**

On a lighter note, Jim told me that one time they steamed in a few miles off shore from an Island that been taken from the Japs. The Gilmer set anchor and the men started to relax for a moment when one of the men, probably Jim, looked through his high powered field glasses and noted a bunch of folks milling around on the beach in question. He sharpened his focus and suddenly discovered that the people he was looking at were Army and Navy nurses on leave. With one shout, everyone who could swim jumped over board and swam all the way to the Island. He said it was glorious. Took the ship's Captain several days to get the mess cleaned up and every body back on board ship.

When the war was over, the Destroyer Gilmer steamed back across the Pacific Ocean and entered San Francisco Bay, passing under the Golden Gate Bridge. Jim got off the ship in his dress Navy Whites, which included his Commander Boards on his shoulders, his combat ribbons on his chest, and his Silver Star for Gallantry in Action.

While on leave in San Francisco, Jim met Maxine Cousins from Ironwood, Michigan. They were married after that and moved back to the black land farm at Rice's Crossing, Texas. There, Jim spent the rest of his life raising Black Brangus cattle and plowing the straightest furrow down the mile or so through his farm you have ever seen. I think one can say that Jim had the war-time medals to prove he "had been there and done that," and didn't need to ever impress anyone about anything again as long as he lived.

Interestingly, Maxine's brother, Ralph Cousins, was a Senior Classman to Jim at Annapolis. Ralph became an airman and served upon the Aircraft Carrier Lexington, which was sunk after the battle of Midway Island. Ralph flew a Dauntless Dive-bomber and during the Battle of Midway Island, he dropped a bomb down the smoke-stack of the Jap Aircraft Carrier Shoto. Ralph went on to become a four star Admiral and was Chief of Staff to Admiral Zumwalt, who was the head of the Joint Chiefs of Staff under either President Reagan or Bush. Ralph and his wife retired and lived at New Port News, Virginia where I had the pleasure of meeting them.

When Ralph retired, the Navy held the retirement ceremonies aboard the Nuclear Aircraft Carrier Nimitz, anchored in New Port News Bay. They had flown a Dauntless Dive-bomber up there from, I think the Confederate Air Forces collection in South Texas, and had it stowed in the hole of the ship. As the ceremonies progressed, they brought the little tiny dive-bomber up on the giant elevator to the level of the flight deck for every one to see. On the fuselage of the plane was painted the name: "Lt. J.G. Ralph Cousins;" Maxine attended the ceremonies, Jim did not. She said everyone cried.

## First Meeting at Our Ranch

In the early 1950s, Dad decided to buy some Brangus cattle from the Slick Foundation ranch near San Antonio. Dad had known Tom Slick for years, and that family was involved in some early Angus/Brahma breeding and the crossbreed that was developed by them was named Brangus. From that work, the Brangus Association was formed and Dad was asked to be on the board of Directors. The breed was destined to be a $5/8s$ $3/8s$ cross, but the 20 or so cows Dad bought were half and half. They were big, black animals, with no horns. They produced a lot of milk, had great looking calves and because of the amount of Braham in them, just a tad snorty.

Jim found out about them and came over to our ranch west of Kyle. Dad sold him several heifers from our herd. Jim had fenced some of the creek area of his farm which grew considerable grass. Jim figured he'd rather graze those areas with cows instead of having to mow it, which would for him be a win/win situation. Get the grass mowed by a great looking cow that produced an even better looking calf which Jim could then take into market at Taylor and make a pile of money.

## Rawls Mesa

In the mean time, I had started college in the fall of 1950 at Sul Ross in Alpine. While there, Dad and I had gone over and visited with some of Dad's old schoolmates from Southwest Normal in San Marcos from before WWI named Mitchell. The Mitchell family was a prominent ranching family in the Trans-Pecos region of deep west Texas, headquarted in and around Marfa, Texas.

During our visit, Mr. Mitchell suggested we take a run down southwest of town about 50 miles because he wanted to introduce Dad to the Rawls family. Mr. Mitchell knew how much we liked to hunt. He thought Dad might like to join him the following year since he hunted there.

So, we took off south of Marfa, toward Presidio, and in about 6 miles hung a left on a dirt road where there was a little wooden sign nailed on a fence post that read: "Casa Piedra, 18 miles." We went flying by there in a big cloud of dust, on past the old ruins at Alameda Creek to a second old sign at a cross road which said Casa Piedra to the right and San Jacinto Ranch to the left. Mr. Mitchell swung left and we went on down in front of San Jacinto Peak. By this time, you could see this very predominant mesa on ahead of us and he told Dad; "There it is, the Rawls Mesa." We turned right at another bunch of falling down ranch signs and drove right up to the base of the mesa where we came to a ranch gate on which were all type of signs attached full of bullet holes, one of which said "Rawls Ranch." Dad got out and unlocked the gate and we drove into the most beautiful 57,000 acres of high desert country we had ever seen.

Mr. Mitchell wound his way up through a canyon until we were on top of the world. We proceeded on in the ranch for about 6-7 miles when we came to the main headquarters of the ranch where Mr. Jack Rawls was waiting for us. There was a landing strip there and he had flown in that morning from Marfa in his tiny Aircoup airplane. It had taken us about an hour and a half to get there, took him about 20 minutes.

That day was the start of a wonderful 18 year relationship between my family and those wonderful folks out there. Jack Rawls invited us to come Mule deer hunting the next fall and we did not leave the ranch until 1968.

The reason I bring all this up was Dad decided to lease the hunting rights from the Rawls in 1951, which was unheard of at the time. Most all Texas ranches in those early days allowed friends and family members to hunt, but the concept we know of today of hunting leases in Texas was non-existent. I do not remember what Dad had to pay but it revolved around the total amount of deer that could be killed (the word now is harvested) on the ranch. It those days, the deer were scarce down there and an individual could only kill one buck mule-deer per year. No mule-deer does were allowed to be killed under state law. I forget if there was a state quota on the bucks or whether Mr. Rawls simply said, "This is all the deer I will allowed to be killed per year." What ever it was, Dad agreed to it and set about lining up friends from the Austin area to join us in the fall of 1951. Jim Hairston was one of the first to sign up. From that day until the day Jim died, we remained the best of friends.

## The Caravan

In those days everyone had an old worn-out jeep of some sort, which we hooked behind what ever we were driving at the time. All of us had gone down to Spillar Welding on South Congress Avenue in Austin and gotten what-ever tow-bars we needed bolted to our jeeps and we were ready. Could be one of our ranch pick-ups or Dr. Raleigh Ross's Pontiac station wagon; what ever would work. We all would decide on a day we were leav-

The Caravan

ing, connect everything that needed to be connected, meet up in Oak Hill or Dripping Springs, or somewhere west and off we would go, in caravan.

US Hwy 290 was a horrible two-lane road running west of Austin and we would snake our way west through Oak Hill, Cedar Valley, Dripping Springs and the crook in the road wouldn't quit until we were finally west of Johnson City, where it finally straighten out a bit. One can still see remnants of the old road which is now Circle Drive west of Oak Hill and pieces of it along Miller Creek west of Henly before one gets to US Hwy 281. We didn't care, we were going hunting!

Jim Hairston did not own a hunting rifle. That's what I said. I asked him one time, why not, and he said, "Well, hell, what can you shoot at across a half a mile of black dirt at Rice's Crossing?"

I answered, "Well, hell, I guess nothing."

You won't believe how the gun issue was solved. Jim drank beer with his buddies down at the cotton-gin at Rice's Crossing every afternoon and one of the boys had a Winchester Model 70, 270. They all knew what day Jim was leaving to go with us, and the night before Jim was to leave, his buddy would slip by Jim's house on FM 973 north of Rice's Crossing, get out of his beat-up old pickup, walk up to Jim's back screen door and prop the gun against the door jam, get in his truck and drive off. Jim never saw him do it in 15 years.

### A Few Stories from Rice's Crossing and Beyond

Besides Jim, there were one or two very interesting characters that lived in and around Rice's Crossing, Texas. Here are two stories Jim told me.

### The Expensive Telephone

Seems one of his old beer drinking buddies never had a phone in his house and decided after many years to get one installed. Everyone thought that was reasonable and somewhat modern. They kidded the fellow every chance they had and then lo and behold after only a few months, he up and had it taken out. Jim said he asked his friend why he had done that and he said, "Too damned expensive!" "What do you mean, expensive?" Jim said, "Couldn't have cost you over $25 to $30 a month." The old timer kinda smiled and said, "Well, last month it cost me about $750!"

Turns out he was calling Hattie's Whore House, way down in south Austin, and having Hattie put one of her girls in a taxi cab and send her all the way out to Rice's Crossing. He said again, "It got too damn expensive, so I had the phone company come over and take it out."

### The Circleville Philosopher

And then there was Henry Fox, the Circleville Philosopher. Henry and Marie Fox lived a few miles north of Rice's Crossing at Circleville. Their place was up on the Gabriel just north of Taylor, Texas; the Gabriel River that is, due north of Rice's Crossing about three beers worth, by Jim's count.

We would all go up there from time to time for supper. Marie was a marvelous cook and we would arrive at their beautiful place on the Gabriel when the Spirit moved all of us. Henry and Marie lived in an old rambling early 1900 farm house that probably had not been painted since just after the Boer War. The first time we went Jim told me not to be surprised by anything, especially the big hole in the dining room wall.

I had no clue what he was talking about, but it seems that Henry had gotten the itch a few years earlier to own a full sized pool table. So he traded for one and managed to move it into the only dining room in the house. As he played his way around the table there was one slight problem. Over in one corner his pool cue would hit the wall every time Henry got over in that position which irritated the hell out of him. So, in typical Henry fashion, he went out into the tool shed, got his double-bitted chopping axe and chopped about a three foot hole in the wall so his pool cue would no longer hit the wall. I was astounded, but the good news out of the renovation project was the hole led into the kitchen and Marie could hand Henry a beer when ever he needed one.

As I said, there were a couple of characters over around Rice's Crossing.

## The Hunt

In the early years, we left from our ranch west of Kyle. So, Jim would crank up real early and come down there and leave his truck at our place. Dad always had a pick-up of some sort and so did I. Dad would have his 1948 hand-made hunting trailer hooked up to his truck and I would have the WWII jeep hooked up to mine. Now, we are only going to be gone about a week but we had enough shit to house and feed an army for a month. AND, the most important stuff was whiskey and bullets. You cannot have too much whiskey and you can never have enough bullets. So, write that down! Oh, and I forgot, nine cases of beer for Jim. Jim was skinny as a rail and smoked a carton of Lucky Strikes a day. Jim said all those months in the water in the South Pacific without his cigs and beer damn near killed him and he was sure as hell not gonna let that happen again.

**Jim on safari**

## The Way It Was

Mule deer season in Texas then was quite different than it is today. It was usually around the Thanksgiving weekend in November or the first weekend of December and only ran for two or three days. The amount of days offered by the Texas Game & Fish Commission was based on census taken of the mule deer population each year, so if they had a good count, four days might be offered. If the Commission had a bad census count for what ever reason, the season might just be for a long weekend.

It has already been noted that the business of leasing ranches in Texas for hunting in the years just after WWII had not begun yet. Even into the middle 1950s, family and friends would simply call up a rancher and ask if they could hunt. So, for Dad to actually agree to pay the Rawls family to hunt on their ranch was a new venture in 1951. It was based on how many deer permits would normally be issued by the state for that particular ranch which in turn would equate to how many hunters would be allowed to hunt. It was around 25 permits.

The Rawls ranch was divided into three Divisions: The headquarters division which was called the Tascatal, consisting of about 25,000-acres; the Holquin division, consisting of around 22,000-acres and the Alazan division, which was down below the mesa, and had about 10,000-acres in it.

The three Rawls men were all alive in 1950. Grandpa Tom Rawls always stayed at the Alazan when he came out from town; Jack Rawls Sr. stayed at the headquarters whenever he flew out there and his son, Jack Rawls, Jr., who was called Junie, lived at the Holquin full time. Dad leased the last two, or about 47,000-acres. No one was allowed to hunt down at Grandpa's.

## People

In those early years, Dad got his life-long friend from Buda, Herman Heep, to basically lease that whole part. Herman had an oil company based out of Austin and used the ranch as a tax write-off. Herman had a twin beech aircraft which could land on the dirt strip up at the headquarters and in the two or three years that he was on the lease, his aircraft was constantly bringing one big-wig or another, including, the then Governor of Texas, Allan Shivers. Herman paid for the bulk of the hunters, but Dad had reserved the right for our family and a few others to always hunt at the same time. And, you will love this; I think the cost per hunter in those first years was $50.00 per hunter.

## On Our Way

Well, you can forget about all those unimportant little details which didn't matter a damn to us, cause we were going hunting. Jim always rode with me in my vehicle. Who ever else was with us that year would ride with Dad. My cousin, Worth Hoskins, who lived on another part of the Kuykendall ranch would come over with his pickup and jeep. Dad's brother, Ike, along with Boone Heep, Herman's nephew and Gerald Montague, store keeper in Buda, always rode with Worth.

We looked like a wagon train in some early black and white movie as we snaked our way out into west Texas, stopping on the hill over looking Roosevelt, Texas west of Junction for a required pee stop, then on to Ft. Stockton. From there on down into Alpine, the home of my ole alma-mater, Sul Ross College, then on into Marfa. There, we re-gassed up everything we had at Maria's Half Price Taco Grocery and Self Service Gas Station. We filled up all our jerry cans for the jeeps; bought bags of tortillas and several cases of Bairds White Bread, all of which would turn green with mold in about 30 minutes if not consumed immediately.

From Marfa, we took off for the ranch causing a dust cloud behind our vehicles that could be seen from space, had anyone been out there to see it. We usually arrived at the Rawls Ranch gate in the late afternoon. By the time we got to the Holquin it would be just about dark.

## Rawls Ranch

Normally, we would arrive at the ranch one to two days before the season opened. That would give us time to settle it, get everything unpacked, get folks parceled out to where ever they were going to sleep, get the rules established with any new folks, etc. It was here also, that Dad split up our bunch. He always sent Cousin Worth and his rowdies over to what was called the Trappers Cabin. The Trappers Cabin was just that; a tin shack where the Government Trapper always camped when he was on the ranch trapping coyotes or some such beasts. It was a perfect place for Cousin Worth, cause he was just one step above a coyote anyway. When Cousin Worth got into the sauce and for that matter, Uncle Ike, Dad's brother, you wanted to be a long way away from there cause those ole boys could get rough. I loved to stay with them from time to time for the adventure but one had to be ready for anything.

## Uncle Bear

Uncle Ike had quit drinking ca.1926 after he rode into Austin from the Kuykendall ranch and commenced to get rip-roaring drunk at the Top Hat Café and Bar down in deep south Austin. It was on old Hwy 81, just north of present day Hill's Café. Turns out in the course of his drunk, he managed to whip about 35 patrons and throw them out through any hole handy including the front door of the establishment. When the Top Hat owner was finally able to get Uncle Ike under control by hosing him down with cold water, he told him two things; *"Don't ever let me see your sorry white ass back in my bar again. And, oh, by the way, when you get time, you might want to jerk out that broke-off pocket-knife blade that is sticking in your skull just up above your eyes."*

Uncle Ike told me later he wondered why he couldn't get his Stetson hat back on. He said he had to use a pair of fencing pliers he had in his saddle bags to get that damn blade out of his skull and he kinda figured he'd quit drinking after that. He said, "Lookee here, Nephew, see that little bitty scar right there," and touched a spot just above his eyes at his hair line. No shit!

Well, his sobriety lasted 24 years until he started coming out to Rawls. My sorry cousin delighted in getting Uncle Ike snockered just for old times sake. I'm here to tell you when he got snockered, they didn't call him Uncle Bear for nothing!

## The 3 a.m. Pee Call

He was real quiet drinker and funny as hell, most of the time. But, he had a real interesting habit. About 3 a.m. of a morning he'd get up out of his bedroll to go outside to take a leak and he thought it would be cordial if everyone in the Trappers Cabin would join him. And I mean everyone. The first time I ever stayed down there I was rousted awake at 3 a.m. by Uncle Ike, who said; "Nephew, go pee." I said, "I don't want to pee, Uncle," and the next thing I knew, my skinny butt was flying out the front door of the cabin, rolling down the side of the hill. After that, I decided maybe I needed to pee after all. Cousin Worth got a big laugh out of that. I usually limited my stays down there to only one or two nights.

On a side note, I asked Uncle Ike one time how come he never had any kids. He said, "Nephew, I'm sterile. I had the mumps when I was down at A&M and they went down on me and my balls swole up about the size of two water melons. When the swelling went down, I had one ball about the size of an English pea and the other'n is just a little bitty son of a bitch."

"Oh," I said.

## Back to the Civilized Camp

Jim Hairston had long since figured out all that shit and he never set foot in the Trappers Cabin. He'd let me go down there for a night or two, knowing I'd be back shortly. He was right. Just how much fun can a feller have?

Jim and I stayed at Rawls until about 1968, or about 18 years. You won't believe why we left? Junie Rawls upped our lease to $80.00 per man, and we said "Up yours, we're out of here." Worse hunting mistake we ever made, and we made several.

We hunted a couple of times on the O-2 Ranch south of Alpine with Harry Carpenter and his son, Johnny. Then went over and hunted a couple of years with Frank Lassiter SE of Marathon, down in Big Canyon. But the really big trips we started taking were to Baggs, Wyoming. I guess we figured we had not driven far enough in our sojourns and Baggs, Wyoming pretty much took the cake.

Jim at Lasaters

## Jim's Gun

Somewhere in the course of things, Jim got embarrassed that he didn't have his own gun so being Jim; he figured he would just make one. So, for about six months, he worked on his new gun in his little shop which was an extension of his over-hanging lean-to garage. He bought a 270 caliber barrel and action from a friend at a gun shop in Taylor. Got himself a gun-stock blank, which was for a Mannlicher-Schoenauer style short rifle, and commenced to put it all together. Jim could carve anything and when he got it finished it was beautiful. Not only had he carved and shaped the wood, but he checkered the fore-arm and the wrist. He installed a four-power Weaver scope on it, went out in the back 40, nailed a target on a fence post and sighted it in. It performed beautifully. He told his friend down at the cotton gin that he appreciated the loan of the other gun over all those years, but he wasn't going to need that gun any more, and "Much obliged."

## The Unloaded Gun

Jim had a very strange habit while hunting. At least, it was strange to me. Jim never kept a shell in the chamber of his gun. He would load or shuck a shell in the chamber when he saw something to shoot at. Man, not me. I was loaded for bear all the time. I complained to him forever to load up but he wouldn't do it. His other habit which directly coincided with the first one, was, when we finished any hunt, and we arrived back at our camp, whatever or wherever it might be, Jim would get out of the jeep, stretch, hold his gun up in the air, and holler, "It's unloaded" and pull the trigger. Well, damn, just the snap alone would make you flinch. I told him until I was blue in the face, to not do that. One of these days that damn thing is gonna be loaded and you are going to be sorry!

He said, "Nah, never gonna happen."

Well, we were camped in a beautiful Aspen grove north of Baggs, Wyoming several years later. We came dragging in just about dark. Dad had a roaring fire going and a pot of stew simmering in the coals. We staggered out of our jeep and I went over and quickly poured myself a civilized drink of Cutty and something. Jim was still trying to unlimber himself from the jeep and as he emerged from it, he walked into the edge of the firelight, and in typical fashion, held his 270 over his head, pointed skyward, and, hollered, "It's unloaded" and pulled the trigger. It was loaded! The damn blast nearly blew me off of the log I was sitting on. The aspen leaves began to fall ever so lightly over our heads from the explosion.

Jim quietly said, "Well, shit!"

Quite a few changes began to occur after 1974. Dr. Raleigh R. Ross and his bunch stopped hunting with us. Dad got very ill in 1974 and died in 1976, so we pretty much hung it up after that.

## The End of the Road

Jim continued to mess with his cows and raise a little cotton. His wife, Maxine, moved to town and Jim didn't go with her. We continued to see one another for parties, suppers and such. When Betty and I got married in 1985, there was no one I'd rather have stand up with me than Jim Hairston, so I asked him to be my best man. He said, "Bud," he had always called me that, "There's nothing that would please me more!" I said, "Me too!"

**Jim, my Best Man**

## The Heart Attack

Around 1986, Jim had a bad heart attack. He went out and got in his little beat-up pick-up and drove himself to Scott and White hospital in Temple. Maxine called Betty out at the ranch and told her. When I got in late that evening, we jumped in our truck and got up there about 1:30 a.m. I walked into the emergency room where they had him all hooked up to every tube imaginable and as I approached his bed he opened his eyes, saw me, and said, "Bud, what the hell are you doing here?" I said, "I figured I'd better come check on you, James." He smiled and replied, "I'm obliged."

A couple of years later, Ken Koock and I ran over there one Sunday to check on him and have a visit. He was in his bathrobe and could barely get around; still puffing on those damn cigarettes which were killing him. We visited for a while and when we got up to leave, I leaned over his bed and hugged him and kissed him on his cheek and told him I'd see him in a few days. He smiled, and said, "Thanks for everything, Bud."

The woman who did his house cleaning and grocery shopping went by the next morning and found him dead on the floor of his bedroom. She had my phone number and called and gave me the news. It was Monday, the 22nd of February, 1988. I asked the family if I might be able to write his obituary and they said I could.

Jim was always a man of good humor and he was unflappable. He never complained about the cold, the wet, the long distances we traveled; Nothing! I guess surviving the Great War had something to do with it. He always savored our times together, as did I. He was in all ways, a gentleman's gentleman. He was well educated, extremely well read, and cared deeply for his fellow man. The conversations we had on our long travels together were very thought provoking and shall always linger in a special spot of my memory.

I loved him dearly, and still do.

W. S. "Bill" Peace

# W. S. "Bill" Peace
## 1923–2004

When David Allen and I were classmates at Kyle High School in the late 1940s, we had all sorts of old beat up antique guns, so we decided to join the Texas Gun Collectors Association. I think David was member number 420 and I was number 421. The association only met once a year. The meetings were normally held in the fancy Shamrock Hotel in Houston. So, in the summer of 1950, we saddled up and went down there. Man, it was something. Here we were with our two or three rusty rifles and one pistol with a sawed off barrel in among nine million of the most beautiful antique firearms you have ever seen. We were in antique gun heaven.

**Young Guns—MEK and David LaVern**

We attended these meetings every year that we could, college and military service years, not withstanding, and almost every time we would go, we'd get to visit with a fellow from East Bernard, Texas named Bill Peace. Bill spoke with a strange accent that we couldn't place until he told us one day that he was deaf. Seems he had lost his hearing from a horrible disease early in the Great War and had to teach himself to read lips. His way of speaking was so different that we thought it was some foreign accent or something. It was not foreign at all; it was just Bill Peace's way of speaking.

After Bill came to grips with his deafness, which took several years, he decided to go to college and chose South West Texas Teacher's College (SWT) at San Marcos. I asked him why he didn't use sign language instead. He said in order to be as normal as he could be, it was imperative to him he be able to talk to people and that's why he struggled for years to learn how to read lips. Not being able to hear the sounds he was uttering was also the reason for his sing/song way of speaking. As he got older, he got so good at reading lips that unless someone was told Bill was deaf, they would never know it.

Bill's father had a furniture factory in East Bernard, Texas that produced office and dormitory style furniture. After graduating from SWT, Bill went to work for his father, later buying the company from him. Bill was so thankful about what the school had done for him during those trying years; the family donated some furniture for a dormitory there.

**Bill and his Sharps rifle collection**

During this period he became very interested in antique guns and the Model that intrigued him the most was the Sharps Rifle. In those first days when we would see one another at the TGCA meetings, Bill would always have a Sharps rifle or two. The next year or so, he would have two or three more. By the middle 1960s, Bill had over 100.

His Sharps collection was so well known by 1965 that he was invited to attend an antique gun show in Las Vegas, Nevada and display his collection. He won Best of Show two years in a row; quite a feat, competing against the best collections in the country.

Even though I did not attend the TGCA shows every year, when I did, Bill and I would always hook up, go for coffee or go have lunch and talk, mostly about hunting. Bill loved to hunt down on the rice prairies around East Bernard, shoot coyotes, geese, and talk about the little white-tailed bucks he had killed.

## Our First Hunt Together

In 1968, we quit the Rawls and decided to go over southeast of Marathon, Texas and hunt with Frank Lassiter in Big Canyon on part of his 75,000 acres. We needed to get a bunch of people together to pay for the lease and it just so happened I attended the gun show that Fall in Houston, and who should I run into, but Bill Peace. We were sitting there shooting the breeze and I was listening to Bill talk about those little piss-ant sized deer he was killing down in the Rice fields when I turned to him and asked; "You wanna go on a real hunt where you can kill a real deer?" He said "What do you mean?" I said, "How about hunting on 30,000 acres down in the edge of the Big Bend of Texas that will cost you $80 for the hunt, plus, you gotta chip in for supplies."

He said; "When do I pack?" And, that was it.

When it came time to leave that November, Bill showed up at the Kyle ranch with his pickup filled with his camping gear and joined us. Our caravan of pick-ups and jeeps looked like a bunch of rag-muffins heading to war.

After that first hunt at Lassiters, Bill leased part of our ranch at Kyle and he hunted there until Dad died in 1976. During this same period, Bill bought a little cabin on Lake Travis where he and his wife, Bobbie, started staying more and more. Eventually they sold their home in East Bernard so they could live on the lake full time.

Knowing how much fun Bill would have with different friends of mine in Austin, and vice versa, I introduced him to Bo and Sue Robinson and all the Robinson clan of Austin White Lime. Bo and his cousin, Spike Robinson were big hunters, and that introduction opened up a whole new world for Bill.

## Learning to Hunt

In those early years, Bill hunted with me out on our ranch in Kyle all the time. I didn't realize until then that Bill had never walk-hunted on his own, ever. What I mean by that is, in his earlier days, Bill would be taken down along the levies in the rice country and dropped off at a deer stand and told to stay put. He had no equilibrium because the disease that caused his deafness had burned out his inner ear and with it, his sense of balance and direction. All of his East Bernard friends knew that and made him stay in one place for fear he would wander off and get lost.

I walk-hunted all the time which was great fun and I wanted Bill to learn how to do it. So, I made Bill walk behind me and hold onto my belt. We would ease through the brush and that way Bill could stay up with me and be in rhythm or sync with me. When I would see a deer, I would freeze, and since Bill was attached to me, he would freeze also. In those early days together Bill had to concentrate and learn how to keep his balance as he walked and hunted at the same time, something most of us take for granted. Because he was always worried about his balance, he would be watching where he was going and I would be looking for the deer.

Then, when we walked up on a buck that he could shoot, I stopped and very slowly showed Bill where the deer was located. And, just as slowly, I got him to ease his rifle up on my shoulder, take aim, and shoot. It was great fun. We did this continually for the first three or four years at the Kyle ranch, until Bill became comfortable walking along side me or close by. By that time, we would work through hand signals so he would know what to do. But, I will tell you one thing, Bill Peace was a marvelous shot. He had no heart-beat wobble that most of us have. When he sighted on an animal, no matter the distance, he could hold his rifle as steady as a rock. I will give you a case in point.

## The Coyote

Since we could not talk on the phone, he would write me all the time about what was going on and whether he thought I needed to come down there for whatever reason.

Well, one day I got a post-card that I needed to get down there... Quick! Seems a friend of his was seeing a bitch coyote and her pup every afternoon about 5 o'clock down along the levies and Bill wanted me to come down so we could kill them. The deal was that we would slip out in the edge of the rice prairie where this fellow had a cattle creep-feeder that looked down toward where the old coyote would appear every afternoon. So, we eased into the little pen that enclosed the feeder and sat down with our rifles stuck through the slates in the fence. I looked down where the levy was and I kid you not, it was a damn mile. I poked Bill in the arm and mouthed, "You mean all the way down there?" He grinned and nodded, yes, and pointed to a spot where he had seen her two days in a row.

Well, durn, I could barely see the spot with the naked eye much less shoot that far and I always considered myself a pretty damn good shot. Course, I never told anybody that I wobbled so bad that if an animal wasn't running I couldn't hit shit.

Anyway, we hadn't been there 30 minutes when Bill poked me and pointed. Sure enough, that old bitch coyote had just poked her head above the levy and was sitting there looking in our direction. I grabbed Bill's 10 power glasses and took a look at her and just as I did, her pup eased up and sat down right beside her. I could see them plain with those 10 powers but when I eased Bill's 30-06 through the slates with the 6 power scope and took a peek at them, it was all I could do just to hold the gun steady enough to see them, much less shoot at them.

Over the years, Bill had migrated from his trusty 30-06 to his 300 Weatherby, which he loved. He kinda reminded me of my crazy cousin, Worth, who thought if a gun wasn't big as a howitzer and didn't kick the shit out of you, it wasn't worth shooting. I hated shooting Dad's 300 because it took a week for my gold fillings in my teeth to quit rattling every time I shot it. But, Bill loved his.

I mouthed to Bill that I just couldn't hold it on them at that distance and as I did he stuck his cannon through the fence and got ready to shoot. I immediately pulled on his sleeve and said lets wait a bit and let them get a little closer. He reluctantly said OK, and just as he did, they were gone. They had sensed us or something as animals in the wild will do and that was that for the day.

We went back to the house, looked at his Sharps Rifles, had a civilized drink (his words) and called it a day. I left the next morning and came back home.

About a week later, I got a postcard. It simply said, GOT HER. Two days later, I got another card which said; GOT THE PUP TOO!

## The Shot

Turns out, Bill had gone back out there and sat each afternoon until that ole bitch finally came back and stuck her head up above that levy. He put the crosshairs of that 300 Weatherby between her eyes and touched "er" off. Bill had the ability to see when and where a bullet hit, like my father. I couldn't. I always blinked as I shot. He told me later, he saw the ring of fire come out of that 300 and also saw the fur fly as the bullet hit her. Bill stepped it off and it was 585 steps. He had hit that coyote directly where he aimed, right between her eyes. Two days later, he paid the pup the same compliment. Same shot, same place, same distance; now, I'm telling you, friends, that is some shooting.

I take a great deal of pride in remembering how I took a novice who could not navigate in the woods, spent two or three years with him in lock-step, until he became a fine hunter. And, what fun we had doing it.

## The Poso Ranch
## El Vado, NM

The Austin Woods and Waters Club, an organization of hunters and fisherman, leased two big, private New Mexico ranches in the early 1970s for its members. One was the 60,000-acre Theis Ranch and the other was the 30,000-acre Poso Ranch. They joined one another and were located SW of Chama, NM, at Vado Lake, NM. The Theis was high game fenced similar to the Chama Land and Cattle Company located at Chama, NM. I make that comment, because high-fences were just coming into being in Texas in those years and were relatively unknown in the western states and rarely used or permitted by the state authorities. High game fences are used in Texas for wild game control where we have no migratory animals like elk and the western mule deer, etc. The Theis and the Chama Land and Cattle Company did theirs to control elk movement or migration so they could manage their herds. It is a practice that is greatly frowned upon by the Game Commissions of the western states and is probably no longer permitted.

Anyway, I got wind from the Austin bunch that a couple of hunting slots were open on the Poso and I asked Bill if he would like to go with me. He said, "Yes." By this time, Bill had bought himself a brand new pick-up with a camper on it for camping. So, we hooked up my jeep and headed out for New Mexico.

The AWWC bunch all stayed at the El Vado Lodge but Bill and I opted to stay on the very north edge of the Poso, about 15–20 miles north of the Lodge. We drove into Chama and bought our permits and it was late afternoon by the time we arrived at our camp site. We unhooked the jeep, drug in some firewood and got our camp ready for our stay. We got out our camp stools, made us a big civilized drink of Bill's Meyers Rum, got a roaring fire lit and settled in for what was going to be a fun experience.

We had arrived one day before the season opened so the next morning we had our breakfast, and headed out to scout out the country. This area of New Mexico is rolling sage with scatted pine and piñon pine timber. It is not a rough country, but you had to stay on the ranch roads because the sagebrush is big, tall and tough and will hang up a jeep big time if you try and run over it. We fooled around all day to get our bearings and never saw another Austin hunter from the lodge.

The good weather broke in the night and when we got up early the next morning, we were greeted to about a foot of snow on the ground. We got our coffee going and just at first light, I looked down below us about one half mile and I could see two orange spots. I drug out my glasses and it turned out to be two hunters from the lodge. Those two crazy sons a bitches had driven half the night to get up near our camp and were hunkered down in the sage about 500 yards directly south of us. We found out later that one of the men had killed a really big mule deer the previous year in that very location. He had convinced his friend that even though we were camped there, they needed to sneak up there and see if they could find another one; was poor sportsmanship on their part and it sure pissed us both off.

## The Full Moon

All good hunters will tell you, try to schedule your hunts in the dark of the moon. Well, shoot, we didn't pay any attention to the damn moon, besides, the hunting season up there was set up by the NM Game Commission, not us. When we got up for our nightly pee-call at about 3 a.m., it was so damn bright you could have read a newspaper. Not only that, but I could see what looked like animals moving just below the camp. I crawled back in the camper and dug out my glasses and there must have been 25 mule-deer down grazing in the sage. I poked Bill and made him get up and look. Man, were we gonna have fun, or what?

Well, damn! You will not believe it, but we drove all over the north part of that 30,000 acres for several days and we did not see shit! Not a single animal. Those damn mule-deer were bedded down so tight in the day-time after having grazed all night that it would have taken a case of dynamite to shake them loose.

After several days of driving, walking, and driving some more, we started back toward camp right at dark. Then right in front of us, about 10 or so deer got up in the sage and crossed the road from our left to our right. One of them was a very nice, thin-horned buck, about 27-inches. We always hunted in open jeeps with the windshield down. I immediately turned off the ignition, tapped Bill on the shoulder and pointed. He stuck that cannon of his across the top of the jeep, took a breath and tapped him. All within a five count. It was a good deer, not a trophy, but a damn good deer. We were elated.

If you were in the woods with us in those days, you'd better get your shot off well below a five count, because if you didn't, you were just whistling Dixie. No disrespect intended; we would have the deer on the ground while most folks were trying to figure out what the hell just happened. We were in the woods all the time shooting at something. I'm not saying that those folks who have come out of their offices on weekends to hunt are not good hunters, I'm simply saying that most just don't have their timing down.

## The Steak Night

Spike Robinson had told us before we started our hunt to be sure and come down to the Lodge on Thursday night because that was steak night. By the time Thursday rolled around, we were pretty much ready for a good steak and would enjoy some of the Austin company, except of course, those two shitheads mentioned a forehand. Ah, hell, by that time we had gotten over it and didn't give a big rats-ass about the incident.

As mentioned, we always hunted in open jeeps and we never gave a damn about the weather, snow I mean, not rain. It probably snowed a foot on us as we hunted that Thursday, so we had commenced to get a tad fortified about dark thirty as we headed down to the lodge. We probably got there about 5:30 or 6:00, but it was flat dark by the time we rolled it and we were covered from head to toe with snow and ice.

We left our cannons in the jeep. Hell, who was gonna steal our guns in a snow storm anyway. We shook as much snow off of us as possible and stepped into the Lodge. Man, it must have been 145-degrees in there, or so we thought. Those boys had a roaring fire going in the fireplace and when we entered the room we must have looked like Dangerous Dan McGrew and his crazy twin brother. The room got very quite, hell, maybe it was an outlaw raid or something. About that time, either Spike or Bo Robinson recognized us and everybody went to hooting and hollering and immediately invited us into the bar to further enhance our consumption.

## The Peace Knife

Bill Peace could make anything. He could make furniture; he could restore anything made out of wood. So, it was not a surprise to me when we started hunting together that he decided he needed to learn how to make hunting knives. He went out and bought some metal blanks used by knife makers for their blades, got some exotic woods, some deer horns and a chuck of elephant ivory or two and went into his garage where he kept all his tools and got started. It wasn't very long until he had two hunting knives made, one for himself and one for me. Mine was a tad rougher than his or should I say, more utilitarian. His was more exotic. He explained to me his reasoning: When I gut a deer and need to break the pelvic bone, I always hunt for a big rock nearby. I set my knife on the pelvic bone seam and pound the hell out of the back of the blade until I have split the bone. He wanted my particular knife to be slightly thicker at the top and much harder, so when he heat treated the blades, he double heated mine for hardness. Bill, on the other hand, took his very sharp, very thin blade and simply cut through the seam. Different strokes.

The hunting folks around Austin had found out how beautiful his knives were and soon the word got out that Bill would sell some and after that he had trouble keeping up with his knife orders. Well, needless to say, you can be assured when we staggered into the bar at the El Vado Lodge that eventful night, we were armed to the teeth, so to speak, with two very fancy Peace knives.

After several rounds of drinks at the bar, everyone started clamoring about Bill's knives, could we see it, etc. So, Bill reaches under about 14 layers of his Eddie Bauer insulated, goose-down jacket and vest and whips out his ivory-handled, engraved hunting knife and slaps it on the bar. There was much oooing and aaahing over such a beautiful item when the owner of the bar, one very grizzled ole man who didn't take shit off of man nor beast and especially a bunch of drunk Texans, said in a very loud voice, "Well, that's nothing but a piece of crap," and whipped out his knife from under the bar and whacked it down next to Bill's.

Bless his heart, Bill understood exactly what just happened, and without missing a beat, picked up the owner's knife with his left hand, turned the blade up, took his knife off of the bar with his right hand and commenced to peel the edge right off of it. I mean all of it! That ole bar-keeps eyes got as big as mama's sauce pans and I just knew he was gonna reach under the bar and pull out his trusty double-barrel 10 gauge and make wall-paper out of all of us when Bill turned the blade upside down and cut the edge back on the old man's knife.

## The Restoration

He then took a paper napkin and sliced it in two pieces to show the bar owner that he had restored the edge to his knife. Everyone started hollering and yelling and the ole bar-keep owner simply smiled and poured us all another drink. The legend of the Bill Peace knife was born that night.

**Peace Knife**

If we ate any steak that night, I'm sorry, I just can't remember. I do remember, however, that when he got ready to leave about mid-night thirty, it was snowing so damn heavy that Spike Robinson prevailed upon me to hook up our open jeep to his Buick and tow the whole kit and caboodle back to our camp. I drug Bill out and poured him into the front seat next to me and somehow made it back to camp. We hadn't even finished peeling off all of our clothes when Bill switched on the over head light in the camper and commenced in no uncertain terms to chew my royal ass out for not letting him ride back to camp in that open jeep, "Just like I went down there," he growled, and with that, rolled over and started snoring his head off.

## An Opportunity Missed

Dadgum it, when I look back on that night, I should have thrown ole Bill in that open jeep and towed him at about 30 mph through all the snow and ice all the way back to camp. Hell, he wouldn't have frozen to death; he had too much anti-freeze in him. But I'll tell you one thing, he'd a-been a "might crisp" by the time we hit camp.

## The End of the Road

Bill and Bobbie have had a house in Santa Fe since the early 1970s. They were on their way up there for an extended stay when Bobbie lost control of the car just outside Big Springs and rolled it over several times. Bill was not wearing his seat belt and was thrown from the vehicle and killed instantly. Betty and I jumped in our truck and went out there early the next morning to check on Bobbie, who miraculously was not hurt in the roll over. We then went by the funeral home to see my old friend for the last time.

What was kinda funny, Bill and I had been by that same funeral home a 1000 times on hunting trips to and from New Mexico and beyond, and every time we drove by it, Bill would laugh, shoot it the finger and say, "You will never catch me dead in that sorry looking place." Sometimes you get what you don't wish for.

"Wish I'd gone to town earlier"

## AN ODE TO BILL PEACE
### 1923—2004

A light breeze blew the news across the edge of the mountains. The crows stopped their squawking; the magpies sat quietly in the spruce trees, and the ravens walked silently along the cliffs over the Chaco Ruins as the word spread. The Man is coming! This was a man who had stood by a thousand wilderness campfires and savored the glow, warmth and camaraderie. Last evening he strode unexpectedly into the glow of the last campfire. It was guarded by the finest Mountain Men that ever held a Hawkins or Sharps rifle. All stood in silent admiration as the man who wore the Grizzly Claw joined them. They nodded their heads in approval. Their quiet voices all spoke in unison as they said, "Welcome, Bill Peace. Welcome home."

So, if you are ever up in the High Country, walking along the rim where the Chama River cascades off the cliffs into the beautiful valley below, and you walk into a large stand of "Quakies" and just get a whiff of a camp fire, stand very still and look where the sun filters its light down through the giant Aspens and strikes the golden leaves on the ground. For you might get a glimpse, ever so briefly, of a giant man standing there, with a big 50 Sharps cradled gently in the crook of his arm, his old Stetson hat ringed with conchos on his head, and a large Grizzly Claw necklace hanging ever so gently around his neck. He will have a radiant smile on his face and he will give you a little nod in recognition. Look quickly, though, my friend, because you will only get one chance, for in the blink of an eye, the wind will change direction and he will be gone.

So, later, as you travel through the Camp Fires of your life, you will be able to tell your children and your grandchildren, that once a long, long time ago, when you were up at the very rim in the high country, walking along an Elk trail and entered a great stand of Quaking Aspens, that there, just for a fleeting moment you caught sight of the man himself, and your life was changed forever.

"A civilized drink."
Here's to you Bill.

—MEK

Dean M. Kilgore

# Dean M. Kilgore
## Austin, Texas

I can't remember when Dean and I first met. I know he did some law work for Mother and me while he was still with McGinnis-Lochridge & Kilgore law firm in Austin. But, it doesn't really matter. What is important is we have been friends for as long as my feeble brain can remember and damn it's been fun.

He and Betty got together years ago over some west Austin real estate; so it's kinda been a mutual admiration society of sorts ever since; Us-uns and them-zuns.

## South Texas Hunt

Dean is a big hunter, especially for quail, and for years he was on some south Texas leases with different friends from the Austin area. The last one was a 10,000-acre place just this side of Eagle Pass where our mutual friend, Tom Searcy from Kyle, was the head honcho.

Tom and Bill Peace had gotten to be good friends over the years; so in the course of things, Tom and Dean figured it might be fun to have the two old outlaws come down at the same time. So Tom invited Bill and Dean invited me. Kind of like an old farts hunting convention and we were the Designated Old Farts!

The Maverick county ranch was just outside Eagle Pass so it was easy to get to. It had a very nice three-bedroom home where we stayed; thought I was in the Waldorf Astoria for a minute, but I got over it. Ain't used to such fine fixins where I've been staying in past years.

Dean and I piddled around the next day; saw quite a few does and some decent bucks. I think their lease was a one-buck affair so we were looking for something that would scare Dean pretty good. It was not my intent to kill anything; I was just the designated backup shooter. It was my job to take the second charge of the beast should circumstances warrant. One cannot be too careful when one is in the bush.

That night Tom threw some prime rib on the grill; Dean made a great tossed salad, and Bill made us all a civilized drink -- or three. We all propped up our feet around the outside campfire and par-took the wonders of an evening on a great south Texas ranch and tried our best not to over embellish some pretty damn good hunting stories.

Dean suggested we swap off the next morning so I could hunt with my ole companion and he and Tom would sneak off some place by themselves and see what they could scare up.

## The Last Hunt

We got up early, downed some coffee and Tom hauled Bill and me out to a big deer-stand we had seen the day before. It was one of those 20-30 foot tall monsters that could easily hold two or more hunters at a time; that is if one could get up and into the son of a bitch. It was kind of a circus for the two of us since it was still dark and we had to climb that sucker with all of our gear. We had our guns, our field-glasses, our water jugs and no telling what else. With all the shit hanging around your neck it's a wonder we didn't fall off the ladder and commit hari-kari right there, whoever Mr. Hari-kari was.

Anyway, with much effort we finally got in that damn thing, got settled and waited for first light. Tom had corned the sendero (cleared area) both ways for probably 300 yards so I had Bill look out the front and I would try and look out the back. We both used 10 power glasses so we began to see the dark shapes of a few deer as they began to come into the corn but it was still too dark to see any horns.

Finally, as the first light began to filter in, we saw one, then two, then three pretty nice 10 point bucks already in the sendero. One was to our rear and the other two were in front. Tom had given Bill his deer tag and told him if he saw a really good one to take him, but please, be damn sure he was a good one. Those deer tags on that lease cost a pretty penny and one needn't get trigger-happy. What did Dean give me? Nothing; shit, my feelings are still hurt.

None of the 10 pointers were anything you wanted to write grandmother about. So we simply watched as they came and went; while they ate some corn; made a run or two at a doe or a competitor buck; and then sauntered off down the cut not to return.

## The Stranger

We had been there about 40 minutes and you could finally see pretty good as the sun started to break through. We were faced south, looking down the cut, which ran over a ridge in front of us and then out of sight. I guess the ridge was about 150 yards from us and was covered with white-brush except where the sendero cut through it.

About this time, all the bucks that we had been glassing had eased off the cleared area and were out of sight. I looked behind us and there was nothing; I turned and looked back down the sendero that way, still nothing. Then, the sun shown on something about 50 yards to the right of the cut on the very edge of the ridge line. I swung my 10 power glasses over on the spot and could just see the head and horns of a hell of a good buck, which had just stuck his head out on the edge of the ridge to see what was going on. He had not approached down the cut like all the 10 pointers; he had eased along the ridge, staying well hidden, and when he got to a spot where he could take a peek, he did. I was lucky I saw him when I did, cause he wasn't going to give me more than a five or ten count, then he'd be gone.

## The Kill

*Shades of our hunt together at El Vado, NM, thirty years previously*; I tapped Bill on the shoulder, and pointed. He swung up his glasses to look and I poked him again and mouthed; "Put your damn glasses down and take him. He's a good one!"

Bill nodded at me, stuck his cannon out the window of the box, took a quick breath and touched it off. I was glassing the buck as he shot and saw him crumple. I wasn't worried about his shot. If Bill Peace ever shot at you, you were one dead son of a bitch and didn't know it.

We attempted to scamper down the 25-foot ladder, however, that turned out to be a bit more of a feat than we had anticipated.

**INSTRUCTIONS**: Unload all guns; turn around and back out the door of the deer blind in question; hopefully with everything you own in the whole world wrapped around you; carefully place one foot on the ladder rung below you; hold on to ladder with both hands; do not release death grip on ladder because the result will not be pretty; slowly lower ones self step by step until one has reached the ground in question some 25-feet below; once on the ground; feel around ones body to be sure one has arrived at ground level with everything one took to the top before daylight. If, in ones opinion, everything is copasetic, then one may continue on with the adventure at hand.

Bill and I immediately went over to the ridge and eased up on one very fine buck. He probably had a 24-inch spread and his horns were heavy. I have killed several 22-inch bucks over the years so I knew Bill had killed a real trophy. I'm not saying he's in the Boone & Crockett Book category of many of the good bucks that are being killed today, but I'm here to tell you, you'll have to work your butt off on a low fenced ranch for many a year to best him. Most of the trophy bucks today are killed on managed game ranches that are high fenced and I'm not knocking them, just saying that to kill one of this category on a low fenced place is not slouchy.

Several years before that, Bill had gotten into video photography and he had his voice activated 9 zillion dollar camera with us; one of the items we had to remove from the 25-foot-high deer blind in question; so I got him to show me how to turn the sucker on and commenced to video Bill and his fine buck.

Both Tom and Dean had heard the shot and came our way immediately to offer any assistance necessary. When Tom saw the buck, he said; "I have seen that deer but was unable to get at shot at him. Man, he is one fine deer!"

We left later that afternoon. Bill made us a copy of the video in the next few weeks and on the box he wrote in pencil: **My Last Hunt!** He was killed a few months later in the car wreck. He was never going to quit hunting and how he knew it was over shall always be a mystery. But, knowing Bill like I did, I understand.

## Bird Shooter

Dean is a Doubles man. When he goes all out, he goes all the way. If one starts to talk about shotguns in front of him, he will drag out in his Mutton Case and very gently pull out his James Lang Imperial 12 gauge, side by side made in London in 1894. Or, if that doesn't ring your bell, then how about two side by sides; one a 1909 John Wilkes (London), and one also a 1909 side by side marked Arthur James Rudd (Norwich). In his words: "Grand guns, all!"

The Rudd is his "go to" duck and pigeon gun, deadly to about 6 kilometers. The Wilkes is best for flushing birds and the Lang best for flighted birds. He tries to make the South American hunt scene as much as he can. Argentina and Uruguay seem to be everyone's favorite now a'days with probably some of the very best wing shooting in the world.

## Occasional Side Trip

He whistled at me a while back and we ran down to Texas Hatters in Lockhart to visit with David, the proprietor. A feller can't last too long without getting himself a new hat from there and Dean was feeling the urge. Seems that Dean had an old 10 X Stetson that had belonged to his father and it needed a tad of refurbishing. Texas Hatters is where one goes for that kind of activity. We walked in the door and howled at David. While Dean was cutting a deal on getting his hat fixed, I spied a fine Panama Straw that had about a four inch brim that was shaped into what is called a Gus Hat. I tried it on and the damn thing fit. Well, durn, didn't mean for that to happen. But that is the risk one runs when one goes into that fine shop.

**Texas Hatters, Lockhart, Texas**

So, we left shortly thereafter with Dean's 10 X being fixed and me sporting a brand new Gus Hat. What made matters even worse was he had done that to me once before when he hollered and said we needed to go down to San Antonio. I said, "Why?" He said, "Cause I need to pick up a pair of boots that are ready at Dave Little's Boot Shop."

So down to San Antonio we go to get his boots. I had never been in Dave Little's shop and, man, you have never seen so many fine boots lining up around the wall in your life. So, what happens? You guessed it. While Dean is picking up his pair of boots, ole you know who here, sat down in the fitting chair and let Mr. Little, "hisself," measure me for a new pair of black ostrich dress boots. Damn, I gotta quit traveling with that Boy.

**Little's Boots, San Antonio, Texas**

There's nothing *un-fine* about Mr. Kilgore. From the best shotguns in the world, to smooth Anejo tequila, my good friend knows and understands the very best. If we could just throw in a gorgeous Argentinean lady for good measure from time to time then life would be perfect, maybe? He is one of those rare individuals that come along very seldom. If one can be friends with him, one better grab a'holt and not let go.

I suppose when and if Dean ever dies, there will be a very simple epitaph on his tombstone that probably reads:

"Here lies Dean Kilgore. He was a good and ethical man and one hell of a feller with a shotgun."

John Henry Faulk in his gunfighter days

# John Henry Faulk

## 1913–1990

I got out of the US Air Force in the summer of 1957, after three years of flying the AT-6 and B-25 aero-planes, and intended to head on down to our ranch in Mexico that Dad and his partner bought a year earlier. But, as fate will have it, my Aunt Marion, Dad's sister, whistled at me and said that she thought it would be good for me to have a tad of European Culture in my résumé before I descended into the bowels of old Mexico. So, she recommended a six week sojourn over the Great Water to the Old Country and handed me a round-trip ticket to travel anywhere in Europe I wanted to go.

Well, one of the best ways to get from Texas to anywhere in Europe just happens to be through New York City, so we got to pondering on who we knew that lived in Yankee land that I could stay with in route. Both Dad and Mother were big buddies of Mary Koock at Green Pastures in south Austin and they knew she had a brother named John Henry Faulk, who just happened to be right on my route to you know where. So dad called Mary Koock; Mary Koock called John Henry; John Henry called dad back, and voilá, I had a place to stay in New York as I passed to and from the Old World.

John Henry was a fabulous story teller and through his connections at the University of Texas and Alan Lomax, who had worked at a CBS radio network in New York, John Henry was able to land a job on WCBS Radio in New York.

He opened his "John Henry Faulk Show" on WCBS Radio on December 17th, 1951. The show, which featured music, political humor, and listener participation, ran for six years. Millions listened to him every evening from 6–7 p.m., live. He could talk Yankee, or he could talk Texan, and the folks all around the New York area loved him. He truly was a Will Rogers of his time.

**New York City**

Well, you know who, got *hisself* a ticket on Braniff Air Lines, and flew into New York City. I boarded a bus to downtown sporting my Stetson hat and was immediately approached by a fine looking gay man, who invited me to his apartment for the evening. Not being of the gay-man persuasion, nor having any knowledge what-so-ever of what the *dear man* had in store for me, I fled to the back of the bus and figured, well, "Welcome to New York." I can't remember if this was before or after the movie Midnight Cowboy with Dustin Hoffman.

John Henry and his wife, Lynn, lived downtown in a high-rise apartment building and welcomed this Texas country boy with open arms. We all sat around that evening and sniffed at each other until we knew who was who, etc.

John Henry suggested that since I only had a couple of days to stay with them, why didn't I plan a tour over to the United Nations Building the next day then come down to the WCBS studio the following evening and be his guest on the show. So, that's what I did.

Johnny's radio show was at 6 PM, so we got up late the next morning, had a leisurely breakfast, after which I whistled up a cab and sauntered down to wherever the UN Building is located.

The cabbie deposited me in this immense parking lot, asked for his money, and pointed at some very large building and said in some strange language, that there was the UN building. Well, as mentioned, for some reason I thought it was important that I wear my Stetson hat on this trip, and of course, I had it planted very securely on my head as I exited the cab.

At the very same moment I fell out of the cab, an enormous tour bus was unloading about 9,000 passengers close by. The folks on the tour bus took one look at the UN Building, then one look at me, and then as if by magic, every one of them did a 90 degree turn and came over to me and asked if I was from Texas. I turned a few shades of red and *allowed as how* I was, and that my name was Marshall Kuykendall. They started ooing and aahing that here was indeed, a real live U. S. Marshal (note the one L) and I spent the next two hours signing autographs as a United States Marshal from Texas. Well, shit, you gotta do what you gotta do!

Since I needed to get back in time to make John Henry's show, I never made it into the UN Building; maybe next trip.

Johnnie's show was live and it was quite an experience to go down to the studios to watch him perform. I think he told me at the time that he had three million listeners. He was on the top of his game.

He told me a funny story that was part and parcel of live studio appearances. He decided to invite some cowboys on his show that were performing in the big rodeo at Madison Square Garden. They yakked about everything and in the course of the interview; John Henry asked them how they prepared or trained for a rodeo and he said they answered in unison: "Whiskey and pussy!"

I left the next day and returned through New York six weeks later. I, again, stayed with him, and he mentioned how sorry he was that I had just missed his favorite niece,

Karen, a daughter of Mary and Chester Koock, who was in Summer Stock Theater in Vermont that summer. I *allowed as how* I was sorry too.

## Blacklisted

John Henry's career at WCBS Radio ended abruptly later when he became a victim of the Cold War and the blacklisting of radio, TV, and Hollywood individuals who were accused of being Communists or Communist sympathizers by Senator Eugene McCarthy of Wisconsin. For a fee, AWARE Incorporated, backed by McCarthy, would investigate the background of any individual in question, and if cleared, they could keep their jobs in the industry. Basically, John Henry told them to go fuck themselves and even though it was never proven by AWARE, nor McCarthy, that he was ever affiliated with the Communist Party, WCBS Radio terminated his employment with the station.

One of the few people in the industry who stood with him in the whole affair was Edward R. Murrow. Nearly everyone one else from those days in radio and early television who had been his friend for years abandoned him; most of them became the foundation for all of the early TV shows to follow. John Henry, who had been extremely popular, would never recover from the blacklisting scandal.

He languished in New York for several more years, but before he left, my wife, Karen and I, flew up for a visit in early April of 1968. (Yes, I married his favorite niece) We were having supper with him and his wife; Robert Ryan, the actor; and Alan Lomax, the folklorist and it just happened to be April 4th, the very day Martin Luther King was assassinated.

When we got the news of the killing that evening it became pure pandemonium in the apartment. Alan Lomax, who had worked among the blacks for years collecting folklore of all sorts, rushed out of the apartment to go down to Black Harlem to be among his brethren. He forgot one tiny little aspect of the explosiveness of the day; He be very white and the folks in Black Harlem be very black and for some unknown reason, they did not take a shine on him being there that particular evening. About midnight, he reappeared at Johnny's apartment with a big red scratch across his throat where one of his black brothers had attempted to cut his throat with a beer opener and failed. Needless to say, brother Alan was slightly deflated over the whole affair.

Karen and I flew out of New York the next day bound for Washington and as we approached Washington, a big part of the city was in flames. We opted to continue on home to Texas, hoping we could *get the hell out of Dodge* before something else bad happened. We did.

John Henry and his new wife, Elizabeth, moved to Texas and lived for a time in West Lake Hills, a suburb west of Austin. Karen and I got a divorce during the same time period and our lives went in different directions. I rarely saw him after that. He got throat cancer in the late 1980s and died in 1990.

We had many good times together in our earlier years.

Ramblin' Jack Elliott

# Ramblin' Jack Elliott

## The Roving Troubadour

Somewhere in the late 1960s, we got a call from John Henry Faulk in New York, who said he was sending some damn long-haired hippie-dude named Ramblin' Jack Elliott by our house in Rollingwood (suburb of Austin), and would we please be nice to him. Well, shit, I hated hippies whether long hair or not, but what do you do?

Sure enough, the following Sunday morning our front door bell chimes and when I open it, there, in the drizzling rain stands a little bitty fellow, with a shit-eating grin on his face, in a Montana sheep-skin coat, a big leather western style cowboy hat stuffed down over heavy curls, round gold-rimmed glasses and a 1924 Martin guitar strung over his shoulder. He holds out his hand and in a very soft voice says, "Hi, I'm Ramblin' Jack Elliott, John Henry told me to stop by if I was in town."

I looked at him and thought, "Well, we are fucked now."

Karen had gotten all our little heathens scrubbed up and was in the process of cooking up a fine brunch/breakfast of eggs and deer sausage. As soon as she had everything ready, we all sat down to a rather awkward brunch as I hummed the tune "God Save Queen Victoria" and looked out the window. A somewhat normal visit took place with Karen and Ramblin' commiserating about her uncle John Henry, New York and other things *Yankee*.

Well, as soon as we had finished, which was not fast enough for me, Jack got up from the table and in his very soft voice said; "If you all don't mind, I would like to play you a little song in honor of this wonderful meal." At that point he went and fetched his antique Martin guitar, swung it over his shoulder and commenced to play the damdest old cowboy music I had ever heard in my entire life. I hate to admit this, but I had a conversion right then and there at 400 Ridgewood Road, Rollingwood, Texas the like of which ain't been seen since Grandma barely missed Grandpa with her 10 gauge double barreled J. C. Petmecky shotgun back in '03!

After that, every time Jack got to playing a gig anywhere close, he always stayed at our house. Then one night in 1969, just about midnight thirty, Jack, who sounded like he was about 14 sheets to the wind, called from Johnny Cash's house in Nashville and told me to get my ass on the next airship, that he was gonna be on the "Johnny Cash TV Show" the next night and he wanted me there. "Damn, Jack, I'm much obliged," I said, "but as bad as I would like to, I just can't make it."

## The Best of the Best

Jack ran away from his Brooklyn, NY home when he was fourteen to join the rodeo circuit and learned his guitar picking from an ole rodeo cowboy who was living in a dugout in Montana. Then in about 1950, he met Woody Guthrie, and lived and traveled with the Guthrie family for many years after that. It was during those years he met John Henry Faulk, who was friends with both Woody and Pete Seegert.

## The Phone Call

**Bob Dylan and Ramblin Jack**

Jack called me out of the blue last year from Carmel, California to see if I was still live and kicking. I *allowed as how* I was and told him not to ever get too close to Austin without giving me a call. He said he would. I then said, "Jack, aren't we about the same age?" He said, "I just turned 80 and still going strong and doing gigs." I answered, "Well, I'm just one step behind you, feeling good and still selling Texas ranches."

We left it on that note; two old friends who met back down a dusty road a long time ago.

He has no enemies, but is intensely
disliked by his friends.

—Oscar Wilde

C. N. Marsh and MEK

# C. N. Marsh
## Granbury, Texas

I don't think I have ever met anyone in my life that could do as many things well as C. N. Marsh. As the movie headlines once stated; he is a man for all seasons. Not only is he probably the best pilot I have ever flown with, but he is superb land man, rancher, and banker. And, if one ever tries to reach him, he's probably out running his bulldozer on one of his ranches over near Coleman, Texas.

He has probably forgotten more about real estate trades than most people learn in a life-time. I remember well, one of the lessons he taught me in land trading. Anytime you are making a trade with a loud-mouth, let him pop his big mouth off about this or that and about the third time he does it, quietly insert a sales contract in his mouth.

Several years ago, I was partners with just such type loud-mouth hot-head on a ranch over in Edwards County. He lost his temper one day and started howling about how he could buy me out any damn time he wanted. It was then I remembered what C. N. had told me. The next howl the son of a bitch made about what he was gonna do to me, I stuck a fucking deed in his mouth. I laugh every time I think about it. Thank you, C. N.

It was C. N. who suggested we all hunt in the Baggs, Wyoming area back in the early 70s. What a great hunt we had and on top of everything, Marshall Jr., who was 12 years old at the time, got to kill his first buck while riding around with the two of us. Junior will be 52 years old his next birthday. Damn, time "*do fly-by*" quickly when one is having fun.

C. N. and I have been friends forever. He lives in north Texas now and I miss the good visits and great hunts we had millenniums ago.

Dr. Raleigh R. Ross

# Dr. Raleigh R. Ross

## Austin, Texas
## 1912–1994

Uncle Raleigh; what a fine fellow he was. He was one of those rare birds that the colder and wetter it got and the further down the dusty road he went, the better he became. And, to top it off, if you poured just a wee bit of sipping whiskey into him, he was one funny son of a bitch.

Raleigh died on Wednesday evening, the 2nd of November 1994. His son, Trip, called me first thing Friday morning to tell me and ask if Betty and I would come up to the Burnet County and help bury him on the ranch the next day. I said we'd be there. Trip said, "Well, do your best." I replied; "You don't have to worry about my best, when it comes to your dad, I'll be there."

Dr. Raleigh R. Ross wasn't really my uncle, but it seemed like it. I'd been calling him that for 40 years. I suspect that in time you can turn anyone into whatever you want and as long as I can remember, he's been Uncle to me.

Some times, you just do things right. Bill Peace and I had been talking for some time about going up to see Raleigh. He'd been sick for a good while. The past spring when his heart stopped we nearly lost him then. So, we figured we'd better get up to the Burnet ranch and have a good visit about the old days, old hunts, old friends and good sipping whiskey.

**MEK and Raleigh**

We gathered up Marshall Jr. and Ken Koock from Green Pastures and spent the afternoon video taping the event and telling all the wild lies we could conjure up. It was a fine time. So many years we had spent together, especially between Raleigh and me. It was good for the soul to reminisce about those times so many years ago.

## West Texas Hunt

Raleigh and his brother, Dr. Abner Ross of Lockhart, had been hunting south of Alpine and they lost their lease in 1953. Uncle was chief surgeon at Brackenridge hospital in Austin and had operated on Dad sometime either in the late 1940s or the early 1950s. They had become good friends. So, when Dad heard they needed a place to hunt, he invited them to join us on Rawls Mesa.

For the next 20 years, we never missed a year hunting together. When we talk of hunting camps and the camaraderie between people that takes place, our relationship has a very special meaning to me. I'm not saying that our camps were bigger, wilder and colder than other folk's camps, but I will say that when you are raised hunting on 57,000 acres of prime west Texas mule deer country, where there were few roads and everything was a-foot, it made a different kind of camp. Where every time you killed a deer, he was always down in a mile-deep canyon; you had to get help and spend two days dragging him out. Only a few special folks could handle it. Raleigh was one of those folks.

Uncle and I have been together in every kind of hunting wreck one can imagine. He was with me when I killed my two 17-shot bucks; he has with me when we were out of water for what seemed like days; he was with me when it was so cold we had to jog for miles just to keep warm; he was with me when the camp burned down and we slept under pieces of roofing tin for a week in the wind and rain; he was with me when the whiskey got so low that we had to mix up everything in camp in a five gallon can just to have a cocktail; he was with me when all the Mexicans in Coahuila swam the Rio Grande river one night just to join the party; he was with me when the dust storm was so bad we had to wear bandanas around our faces to keep the dirt out; he was with me when we trailed up numerous wounded bucks. We never let one get away.

There are very few folks on this planet that could operate in the hunting camps we used to have and maintain their sense of humor, much less direction. Uncle was one of those few men who only got better when the going got worse. There are only one or two of us left from those wild days. The list is getting kinda short.

## Some Hunting and Camp Fire Tales

Raleigh got us all a father/son hunt on Jack Bowman's ranch at Big Wells in about 1970 when we burned his camp-house down. Didn't mean to, mind you, it just happened. That was the time that Raleigh uttered his famous line: "Let's all go over and confess what we have done or go home the back way and never speak to the no good son of a bitch again," meaning Jack Bowman, of course. We relented and went over and confessed. Afterwards Jack laughed and said, "Shit, Raleigh, you could've seen the smoke from Laredo.

## Mr. California and the Near Miss

Dad and Raleigh hunted in Idaho on a couple of occasions back in the 60's. Every body had their own guide, or white-hunter, as Raleigh called them.

One day Raleigh and his white-hunter were out in a pretty good snow storm and ran up on a big bull elk. Raleigh took a whack at him and knocked him down. The ole bull wallowed around a minute, rolled over and took off. Raleigh was unable to get a second shot at him.

He and the white-hunter waited a bit, then started to follow the blood trail to see if they could get another shot. They hadn't gone a half a mile when they ran up on a lost hunter from California, hence the name, who fell in with them. Raleigh said Mr. California was sporting a brand new .300 Weatherby and was all decked out in his Eddie Bauer outfit and as Raleigh put it, didn't know shit from shinola; didn't know where his camp was, didn't know where he was; nothing!

Off they went again, still following the trail of the wounded elk, a blood spot here and there, walking in deep snow. The white hunter was in front, Raleigh was in the middle and Mr. California was in drag.

They hadn't gone a half a mile when there was the damndest explosion you have ever heard. Powdered snow flew all over Raleigh and the guide. Seems that Mr. California had been walking behind them the whole time with his cannon off safety, had obviously stumbled, farted, and pulled the trigger at the same time. The bullet passed between Raleigh's legs and just to one side of the white hunter; blowing snow every where. The two of them stood in absolute shock silence for a moment, then the guide felt himself all over to see if he had acquired any extra holes and said, "You know Doc, that bullet could've gone plumb through you and kilt the shit out of me."

With that, they turned around and started back toward camp. Raleigh said he told California he hoped he never found his camp and got his sorry butt frozen solid for good measure.

## The Meriwether Ranch and the White Mule

Raleigh was hunting on the Meriwether ranch a couple of years before they joined us on the Rawls ranch. The ranch lay just south of old Hwy 90 between Marathon and Alpine.

The country was pretty rough and you had to walk-hunt every bit of it. Somewhere in the scheme of things they had gotten hold of a white mule to use as a pack animal when and if they killed anything.

A couple of days into the hunt, they were out and about, white mule in tow, when they heard some shots just over a hill from them. Raleigh said no one else was supposed to be on the place, so they hustled over the hill and ran up on a poacher who had just killed a pretty decent buck. The hunter was pretty surprised to be caught and didn't seem to want to cause them any trouble but under the circumstances just wanted to get the hell out of there. But, could he please take the deer he had just poached? Raleigh asked him; How in the hell are you gonna do that?" Mr. Poacher pointed at the white mule.

Raleigh said; "Well, shit, first you poach on our place, second you kill one of our deer and third, you got the gall to want to borrow our god-damned white mule."

"Uh huh," replied the feller.

## Kicked in the Orange

Well, they all got together and started trying to load the deer on the white mule when Mr. Mule kicked the dog shit out of the poacher, hitting right in his big fat belly. Raleigh said the ole boy lay moaning on the ground and crying that he was dying and that "his guts was busted."

Raleigh being the outstanding surgeon that he was, rolled the poacher over to see if he was gonna die or not. After examining him very carefully, stood straight up, put his glasses back on and said, "Shit, you aren't gonna die, the damn mule just kicked you in the fucking orange."

Seems our poacher friend was wearing one of those sweat-shirts that had the little warming pouch in front and he had stuffed three oranges in there and that's where ole Whitie had kicked him. Poacher-man had felt all that goo and gunk running down his fat belly and thought for sure he was dead.

## The Executive Pissing Contest

Normally when one hears that someone got into a pissing contest, it usually involves one hell of fight. Well, not in this story.

Here we are, a bunch of highly educated doctors, lawyers, ranchers and Indian Chiefs, and what do we talk about over a roaring fire and a little sipping whiskey late one night at a hunting camp in Bum-Fuck, Wyoming? Who can piss the furthest! Well, there was a reason. One's honor was at stake.

A few days previous to this intellectual discussion, Raleigh went into Craig, Colorado late one afternoon for supplies. It got a tad late so he swung by the local pub to fortify *hisself* with a beer or three, before returning with our supplies.

The establishment was rather dark and dreary so Raleigh sat at the bar and commenced to down a few while visiting with one of the locals and just about the ugliest woman bar-keep he had ever seen. After a few beers, Raleigh got up to go take a leak when the local made some comment like, "Sure hope you can piss far enough to hit the urinal." Raleigh turned and replied, "Not to worry, I can handle it." The local retorted, "Sure hope so!" At which time, Uncle Raleigh said, "Shit, I can piss over your truck, if I wanted to." The local snorted, "Bet your Texas ass $100 you can't." With that, they all flew out the front door to commence the contest.

They walked right out to the subjects truck, whipped out their necessary tools and commenced to try and piss over it. They were doing a pretty decent job of it, when a loud bang was heard as the bar door slammed open. Out charged the barkeep, in her old beat-up cowboy boots and a rather short dress. She came flying up to the boys hollering, "Get the hell out of my way!" When she got to within about 6 feet of the old pickup truck, she turned sideways, pulled up her dress and cocked one leg up in the air, cowboy boot and all. And, as Raleigh reported, "Pissed plumb over the god-damn truck."

Raleigh looked at the ole gal, looked at the ole local, looked at the ole truck, and said, "Well, fuck me," reached in his pocket, pulled out a $100 bill, slapped it on the hood of the truck in question; got in his vehicle and came back to camp with his tail between his legs.

Bested by a woman in a pissing contest, and an ugly woman at that! We all howled with laughter over that story.

## The Company Ranch

Raleigh bought an 8,000-acre cedar-break called the Company Ranch in Burnet County in about 1965 through the Trust Department of the Capital National Bank of Austin for $50.00 per acre. The ranch is located on top of the high ridge overlooking the whole world just north east of Marble Falls and slightly east of Mormon Falls. It is one rough, mean son of a bitch and is just barely holding the world together. He spent the rest of his life trying to flatten out that sorry ole place by running his own bulldozer back and forth over as much of it as he could, but I'm not sure it helped.

Raleigh built his home on the very top of the ridge. In it, he built a bell-tower and every Thanksgiving when we were up there, he would get up and ring the bell to let everyone in about 13 counties know that he was having a party. It was glorious.

Raleigh had several heart attacks and the last one in 1994 got him. The funeral home had dug a hole in solid rock about 50 yards behind his house, and the night before the get-together, it rained about a foot. The damn hole filled almost to the top. That part of the country had been dry so long that a good rain was welcome. Someone got a water pump and pumped out the hole so we could get his casket to quit floating to the top every time we tried to drop it in the hole. Raleigh would have loved it.

I walked over to the hearse that fine, cold, crisp, sunshiny day and helped pass my friend, in his beautiful box, with no handles from one friend to another as we laid him in that place where he wanted to be. Then we rang his great bell, up in the bell tower, on top of his mountain hide-away that he loved so well and said goodbye.

Raleigh left me his favorite rifle that he had used all over the world. It was a beat up 30-06 Remington Pump. The forearm was so worn down that it almost needed to be replaced.

Thank you, Uncle. It was one fine dusty road we traveled together, wasn't it? I'd do it again in a heart beat.

Ken R. Hagan

# Ken R. Hagan

## Uvalde, Texas

**K**enneth Ray! Damn, what good times we had together years ago. Ken and I met in the early 1960s when we moved from the Kyle ranch into town. A.D. Stenger built us both a house; mine on Ridgewood Road and Ken's on Sugar Shack.

Ken was originally from Hocheim, Texas just west of Yoakum. His dad, C. O. Hagan was a land trader, early day bracero contractor, and insurance company owner.

Ken and I were best buddies for years and we owned a bunch of real estate together. One piece was the 1848 rock house located at 105 Neches Street in Austin where the convention center is now located. It was later moved up on 4th and Red River close to the Waterloo Compound. Ken and I bought it through old man, A. L. Moyers, who handled all the real estate in Austin for the Josephs and the Attals at the time. We paid $14,000 for it and not a single bank nor insurance company would touch it since it was located east of Congress Avenue and below 6th street.

The damn thing was pink stucco and had all kind of shit stacked in the front yard at the time, like twisted car bumpers and antique commodes with flowers in them. The renter at the time called it *yard-art*. We called it what it was: *SHIT*.

He and I rounded up a covey of "exchange students" looking for work at the time to camp in the house and chip off that horrible crap troweled on there by one of the previous renters. We just about had it all removed, when some enterprising Austin policeman happened by one day and hauled all their asses off to jail because they were *Illegals*.

It was remodeled over the next year or so and in 1974 it was sold to an architectal firm for about $31,000.00. I figured we had killed them. I'm sure, when whoever had it later on sold the location to the Austin Convention Center, they probably got nine million.

Kenneth loved the horse races so we bought a house in Ruidoso, NM to be near the race track. Later, we bought 100 acres behind Appaloosa Run off of FM 1826, where we built a bunch of really wonderfully funky houses. So, funky, that my dear friends, Joe and Sharon Ely, decided they had to have mine and are still in it to this day.

The Wild Bunch

MEK after bull cutting

## Working Cattle
## And The Big Ball Kicking

Our friend H. C. Carter of Austin, had 1,500 acres or so on Lake Austin just off FM 620. He and Ken made a deal to partner some cattle there. Twice a year we would all get together and have a big round-up. Out of about 100 mama cows, they'd end up with about 25 bull calves. We would spend all day rounding them all up and separating the bull calves into one corral and the heifer calves into another. As soon as we had that done we'd get in the pen on foot with those bull calves and that is when the fun began.

There were only about four or five of us that knew how to work and mark the bull calves. This entails getting into the pen on foot, grabbing a calf, throwing him down and while he is down, someone, normally Ken, castrates him and marks his ear. I was a "header" and H.C. or his brother, Buddy, were "tailers."It was a hell of a lot of fun and a lot of work. So, in order to make it more interesting, friends were invited to help out. On one such occasion, an Austin City Councilman was invited to partake in the festivities.

We had worked about a half a dozen of the bigger calves first and were taking a breather. I pointed at a big black Angus calve and said "Let's get him next." He was about the last really big one and we were getting kinda worn down from all the excitement. What we would do is all get in the pen together and push them into a corner. I would ease in among them and grab the calf we were after around the head and start to try and twist his head off. Then one of the helpers would rush in and grab him by the tail and jerk him down. The City Councilman wanted to be the next "tailer." I hadn't any more than gotten a hold of this big black calf when I heard this big ka-whop and looked around and Mr. City Councilman was lying on the ground curled up in a big ball unable to move.

Rule number one is never just walk straight up to a calf. Always kinda saddle in sideways cause he's libel to kick the shit out of you. It's better to be kicked on your chaps on the side of your leg than to get kicked in the balls. Well, the feller didn't know that and he just walked right up behind that calf as I was holding on his head. The calf was trying to figure out what in the hell was happening and even though I had a pretty good hold on him, he still heard or felt something behind him and he let fly a humdinger of a kick. It caught Mr. City Councilman flush in the crotch with a pop that could've been heard up on FM 620 and damn near killed him. I turned the calf loose and ran over and try and help him up but he was lying in a ball, frozen stiff from the *lick* and not able to get his breath. It took several of us pounding on his back to finally get him to breathe. We drug him out of the corral over to a horse trough, sat him down and started wiping his face with cold water. It took nearly thirty minutes for him to be able to stand, much less talk. That bull calf had done a real number on him. While us cowboys kinda chuckled about it afterwards, I can assure you it was no chuckling matter for our guest. Bet he went home and *allowed as how* he didn't ever want to get in a pen with a bunch of bull calves again as long as he lived.

## The Bucking Bull

A few days later Ken called me to say that one of Steiner's bucking bulls had swum Lake Austin and was over among the cows. Tommy Steiner owned a big ranch on the east side of Lake Austin just across from H. C.'s place and had it stocked with about 50 bucking bulls. Obviously the bull had heard all the bawling and commotion from our roundup and decided to pay a visit. Tommy was one of the premier stockman for the National Rodeo Association and he furnished "bucking stock" (bulls and horses) for all the major rodeos across the US of A.

This Brahman bull must have weighed 2,000 pounds and when Ken tried to pen him in the puny corrals that existed on the ranch, he would just snort and brush Ken and his horse aside and trot back down among the cows. After a couple of tries, Ken realized that wasn't working so got on the phone and called over to the Steiner ranch. He told the cow-hand who answered that one of his bulls was over visiting. The cow-hand told Ken not to worry that he would be over there directly and fetch him back.

About thirty minutes later this little bronc-busting cowboy showed up with his pickup pulling a cattle trailer in which he had a big, rangy, bay, cowpony about 16 hands high. Ken said this small bow-legged feller got out, hollered "Hi 'D," unloaded that big bay and hit a little lope down to where the bull was located. In about 20 minutes here they came in a slow trot up to where the rig was parked. Just as the bull passed the downed tail-gate on that trailer, Ken said that cowboy dropped a loop on the 2,000-pound bull and before he could blink, jerked that son of a bitch flat as a pancake. He then flipped the rope over the side of the trailer and as the big old bull was getting his feet, snatched him plumb up into that trailer. He stepped off that bay while the rope was taut and ran around and shut the tail-gate. He hopped back up on the big Bay, got some slack in the rope, flipped it off, jumped down, tied the bay to a cedar bush, told Ken, "Much obliged," got in his truck and drove off. Ken said it was the damndest bunch of cowboying he'd ever seen and Ken was no slouch as a cowboy "hisself." He said, the little feller never broke a sweat.

## The Big Split

Sometime in the late 1980s, Hagan had had enough of the Austin scene, so he saddled up his old horse, figuratively speaking, rode outside the gate of the Austin corral, turned in his saddle, shot us all the finger, and said, "Fuck it, I'm out of here," and split for south Texas, bought a neat ranch at Batesville and started trading in wild cows and possibly stray women and we haven't seen him since.

I guess when the twig snaps, it's over; or maybe it's when the branch breaks; or maybe it was all the whiskey we drank together; or maybe it was all the x-wives he had; or maybe it's the time he poured gasoline in the *two-holer* and someone dropped a cigarette in the other hole; or maybe he just blew a fuse—hell, I don't know.

However, on third thought, maybe it was the memory of the time one of his girl friends drove her brand new Cadillac El Dorado convertible completely through a south Austin apartment complex looking for him. *I mean all the way through it.* She started in the parking lot on one side and ended up in the parking lot behind the complex.

When I got with him I asked, "My God, Kenneth Ray, what in the hell happened?" He said, "Well, you won't believe this, but she damn near killed me." Then he got a real big shit-eating grin on his face and said; "After I shook all the sheet-rock and dust off of me, I realized she had missed me by just this much," and held up his thumb and forefinger about an inch apart.

Then he said, "You know, MK, if you are ever gonna get a secret love-nest in an apartment complex, by God, always get it on the god-damned second floor."

*No shit! Really?!*

I guess he figured when it was time to split, one might as well do it in style. He definitely did that. We had many good times together and there are some mighty fine memories stuck back there somewhere in the recesses of my mind. But I do know one thing for certain;

Kenneth Ray is someone you could *always ride the river with*; no cliché intended.

His mother should have thrown him
away and kept the stork.

—Mae West

Carol, MEK and Ken Koock

# Ken L. Koock
## Austin, Texas

One of the great things that happened to me when I got married in 1959 was that I got Ken Koock as my brother in law. The Spanish word for brother in law is *cunado*, or Coonie for short. Well, once a Coonie, always a Coonie is our motto.

Man, we have done some crazy shit together in the last 50 something years; wine, women, song, boats, airplanes, hunting, travel, you name it and we have done it. And we have done it with gusto. The good news about Ken being born and raised at Green Pastures in south Austin was we never had to go hungry. Any time he showed up for us to do anything, he'd always bring about half the kitchen with him.

We would look at a ranch in Mexico one week and go hunting the next. Here are some tales that tell it all.

### Mexico

Coonie and I bought a brand new Cessna 182 Skylane from an old man in Temple for $11,000. We had an older one before that, got in it and flew up to Temple and made the deal. The damn airplane still had all the smell of a new car; it was so new the ashtrays in the back seat were still taped shut. The only minor problem it had, and this is our private joke, were the long range gas tanks in it that would allow us fly longer than our *bladders* could take it. But, if you are pilot, the only time you can ever have too much gas in an airplane is when the damn thing catches on fire.

By this time, I had returned to Texas from our ranch in Coahuila, Mexico with quite a bit of flying time in a Cessna 182, which by far, was my favorite ranch airplane. So, when I got a call to look at a 25,000-acre ranch in the Burros Mountains southwest of Del Rio/Villa Acuna, I whistled up Coonie and my friend Bill Peace to go with me and off we all went.

Not only was the owner thinking about selling it but he also told me we could hunt for some black bear while we were there. We still had our landing strip on the ranch west of Kyle, near the Hays City store, so I told both fellows to meet out there.

We flew into Eagle Pass and picked up the foreman and a horse wrangler and headed out nearly due west into the late setting sun. We were loaded to the gills with five people on board and all our shit, but one thing about the Skylane, if you could get the damn doors shut, the son of a bitch would fly. About the only thing that would over-load it were sacks of concrete.

## The Mexican Ranch

I flew down to Eagle Pass and Ken did the flying into the ranch. The owner sat up front to tell Ken which way to go and I sat in the back so I could visit with the wrangler and Bill Peace. As mentioned, it was late in the day, real dusty and we were flying right into the setting sun. You couldn't see shit from the glare on the windshield.

The country up river from Eagle Pass and inland from Acuna, Mexico is flat level mesquite country until you hit the Burros Mountains about 50 miles west southwest of Acuna. On a real clear day, if you are driving on old Hwy 90 from Del Rio toward Langtry and look to the SW, you can barely see the tops of the Burros. The flat land area is pretty much grease-wood and mesquite brush but as soon as you hit the mountains, it changes immediately to upper black grama grass country with scatted pine and piñon pines on the hill sides. It is beautiful.

Any-hoo, we are rocking along not seeing shit, when the wrangler, who is over on the far right side leans up and whispers to his boss in the front seat, "¿Oiga, jefy, estamose bien perdido, No?" Well, I heard what he said, and since I was sitting right behind Coonie, I leaned up and whispered to him and said, "No, we are not lost, but give me a bit of right rudder for a minute so I can look out my side window." I knew the country well, having flown into it with Max Michaelis many times in years past. So, when he gave me a bit of a look, sure enough, I could barely see the outline of the approaching Burros. I knew from the course we were flying that we would be on them in a minute or two and would need to get down and fly right up one the deep canyons, so I told Coonie to take plane down which he did. As soon as we got the plane down low, the glare off the setting sun went away because the sun was behind the Burros and suddenly we could see where we were, which was right on top of the canyon we needed to be in.

The owner had told us the ranch was real close, that the strip ran up hill and a small set of ranch improvements would be on the left side of the canyon. We hadn't gone a mile until Coonie saw it, dropped full flaps and in we went. The grass strip was smooth as glass and ran up hill so we had no trouble stopping the airplane. I did make a note however, that there was a big mountain ridge right west of the house, and figured no matter which way the wind was blowing when we got ready to leave two days hence, that we would have to take off down hill or we wouldn't make it.

The valley was beautiful, with a neat little ranch house and corrals off to one side and hills that were covered with pine trees. The elevation was about 4000 feet, pretty good since Del Rio is about 750 feet. So, you can see what I mean about flying into some pretty good mountains that one would never expect. One minute you are tooling along in the flats and then you aren't!

Mexican owners rarely stay on their ranches. They all live in town. So, one has to take what ever you are going to eat or drink or you are up shit-creek for provisions. This beautiful place was no exception, so we had everything we needed, down to Bill's Myers

Rum. We got out of the airplane right at dusk, hauled all our stuff into the house, got the propane stoves and lanterns lit and got ready to enjoy ourselves a civilized drink, when I noticed three five gallon plastic bottles full of whiskey standing over in one corner of the living room. One was Johnny Walker Red Label, one was Cutty Sark Scotch whiskey (my favorite) and last one was Bacardi Rum. I mean labeled and all. *Whiskey Heaven!*

Well, I fell on that five gallon jug of Cutty Sark like a chi-chi bird on a June-bug to see what kind of dent I could make in it. After several Mason jars full of scotch were consumed, it seems the only dent that appeared was the dent in the side of my head. You might think you can drink all the whiskey out of a five gallon jug but even after everything I tried, I don't think I lowered that whiskey level one damn inch. But, man it was fun to try; that is until sun-up.

## The Roosters and the Bullet Holes

We all staggered out of bed about daylight thirty the next morning to commence our day of adventure. As soon as I got my eyes somewhat focused, which took a we bit of doing, helped along, of course, by some really stout coffee, I noticed a bunch of bullet holes in the front windows of the house. I eased over to get a better look and just as I did, a couple of roosters and hens came hippy-hopping by. I say hippy-hopping because one of the big roosters was missing about half of his foot on one side and what looked like about one or two toes on the other. I turned to the foreman and asked, "¿Oiga, que paso con el gallo?" (What the hell happened to the rooster?)

I laugh as I remember this: He said, "Cuando el dueno es aqui que se emborracha y cuando se despierta el tiene un gran dolor de su cabeza. Cuando ese gallo empieza a cantar lo primero en la manana se enoja. El consigue su 45 atomatic empieza a dispara a traves de la ventana del frente tratando de matarlo el Cabron."

Turns out the owner had not been successful in killing the rooster in question, but he had nicked him one or twice, hence the missing feet and toes. The lesson learned from the night before, if there was one, was that we were damn glad the owner wasn't with us or the bullets might have been flying that particular morning for sure.

Coonie whipped out one of his marvelous breakfasts of chorizo y huevos as we waited on the horse wrangler to get our mounts ready. There were no vehicles at the ranch and the plan was to take a pretty look at the place by horse-back. Bill Peace hated having to ride but we coerced him into it. Telling him that wonders awaited to be experienced and he needed to get his butt in gear, literally.

This part of northern Coahuila, Mexico is really very beautiful. Soft, grama grass valleys with steep ridges covered with live-oak brush and scattered pine trees. We followed the wrangler on a big loop over the top of the ridge and down into the valley beyond. I was behind the Vaquero, followed by Bill Peace and Kenneth brought up the rear.

At lunch time, we stopped on one of the high vista points of the 25,000-acres where we ate our egg and chorizo filled tortillas that we had rolled up and stuffed in our saddle bags. We spent most of the day on this big loop; saw a few mule deer scampering away from us, but no bear. We got back into the ranch house just before dark.

We were a tad more subdued on this evening and for some unknown reason, none of us attacked the five gallons jugs. I think we all learned our lesson, at least for a time. A cold front had blown it late that afternoon, so we built a big roaring fire in the fireplace and enjoyed the beautiful setting. Not many folks get the opportunity to see this part of Mexico.

It was our plan to fly out the following morning. I was not real happy with the north wind blowing right down the airstrip the wrong way. The strip was very short and I was obliged to take off down hill to the south, since the other way was not an option. I told everyone to be ready to go at first light, hoping the wind might have lain by then.

## The Downwind Takeoff

Kenneth had us all up early with our breakfast ready. I got my coffee and walked outside to discover that if anything, the wind was blowing stronger downhill that it had the night before. I was not worried that I could get the airplane off the ground, but at 4,000 feet elevation and a tailwind blowing like hell; it did make the takeoff a tad trickier. One thing that helped was the fact that the vaqueros weren't going back with us, so it would just be me, Coonie, and Bill Peace. And, we had burned off considerable fuel, so weight was not going to be a problem.

Like all ranch airstrips, this one had a fence at the lower end of it and to help matters even further, the canyon made a sharp turn just beyond the fence. I have a lot of flying time in northern Mexico and had gotten to a point where I paid close attention to those little details. Such was the joy of flying in the Mexican mountains.

One thing I did not like about winter flying there was the fact that the wind howled around those damn mountains and canyons and the turbulence was fierce; nothing like flying in the summer time. One moment you would have a headwind, the next moment a tailwind; sure played havoc with you when you were too close to the ground. The winter turbulence could shake you up pretty good and make your teeth rattle, not to mention what it did to the airplane. I have been full power on and full power off on several occasions just trying to keep the airplane in the air.

We downed our coffee, threw all our shit in the plane, told the vaqueros *muchas gracious* and saddled up. Ken got in front with me and Bill got in the back. I cranked up and taxied into the wind and got up just as far as the dirt strip would allow; turned the plane downwind and downhill and wound up the rubber band on that 230 Continental engine just as tight as I could wind it, turned and nodded at the boys and cut "*er*" loose.

I won't bore you with all the aeronautics' stuff, but any time you take off down wind, you use more runway than normal because the airplane does not want to fly. On top of that, while the 182 had good power, it was not turbo'd, and we were taking off at 4000 feet elevation. That meant we were going to use even more airstrip than I liked. While most ranch barbed-wire ranch fences are only about 5 feet high, when you are approaching one at the end of the airstrip at about 80 to 100 mph and your airplane is still not responding, the damn thing looks like its 20 feet tall.

**Cessna 182 Skylane**

The strip probably had about 2,000 feet total, fence to fence, but it was smooth as glass and that helped a lot. By the time I was half way down, which took about five seconds, the plane wasn't even up off its shocks yet. I had put 10 degrees of flaps down before I started and when I felt we were not getting airborne, I reached down and pulled on another 10 degrees. By that time, we were long since committed. I took one more hard look at the looming barbed wire fence and realized it was either fly or *Katy bar the bedroom door.*

I had quite a bit of flying time on ranches in northern Mexico and I was pretty good. On top of that, I had lots of respect for those damn mountains. The Mexicans have a wonderful saying about them, which says something like this; "Be careful where you fly in northern Mexico, because the hills are full of rocks."

As soon as I dragged on the second 10 degrees of flaps I horsed the column back in my lap and made that sucker fly whether it wanted to or not. Man, the stall warning horn started howling as soon as we broke ground and the airplane was pitching and jumping just like a bronc coming out of a bucking chute. At the same time, the damn tail must have yawed 30 degrees from the tail wind. I think we passed about 3 feet over that fence at the end of the strip and I'm here to tell you, neighbor, we were *trucking.*

We got to the end of the canyon and I started to make the slight turn to the left when we hit a down-draft that literally banged our heads against the ceiling, threw all our luggage up in the air and took us almost to the ground. I horsed the yoke back even further which really got the attention of the stall warning horn and just as I did, we hit an up-draft that nearly pulled the wings off the airplane. With that assist, we went howling up and over the ridge in front of us into the clear. The most important thing to keep in mind when getting catapulted into space down there was be damn sure to keep the nose of the aircraft in question pointed in the right direction. *Shit!* Was that fun or what?

I looked over at Coonie and he was grinning as he gave me the thumbs up. I looked back at Bill and he wiped his brow with his handkerchief and then shot me the other finger, the middle one I mean, but, with a big grin attached.

Damn, I hate flying in the northern Mexico Mountains in the winter.

## The Colorado Hunt

Ken went with us on most of our hunting trips, one to Lassiters, one to Sevolla, NM and one to Lake City, Colorado.

The entire bunch went to Lake City that year; Ken, Dad, Raleigh, Bill Peace, Jim Hairston, and me, of course, with another Mexican thrown in for good measure.

Somebody had talked to the owner of the ranch where we were going to hunt and we were able to stay in one of his log cabins. It turned out to be one of the best hunting camps we ever had. The area was at the edge of the Rocky Mountains and we were hunting at about 8,000 feet elevation. This put us in a bit of sage on the lower part; pine trees in the middle and lots of aspen up along the ridges; country typical of the Lake City, Colorado area and quite beautiful.

## The Watch Dog

Funny what pops in your mind as you wander through these old memories, but we had to drive two or three miles every morning before day light to get to our hunting country. In so doing, we drove through the yard and corrals of the owner and every time we did, this ole mongrel watch dog, of some kind, would rush out of the barn and try and chew the damn tires off our jeep.

A few days and many chewings, gnawings, growlings and snarlings later, we were finished with the days hunt, had every body loaded up and were heading back to camp. We, of course, had to drive back through the pole corrals and the gate posts of the corrals were narrow and barely wide enough for us to get through. Just as we approached the gate, Mr. Cur dog came flying out of the barn to do his duty and started gnawing the hell out of my left front tire. About that time, Coonie hollered, "Git him!" I eased the front of the jeep over to where I was going to scrape that big gate post, all the while *you know who* was doing *you know what!*

Well, I skimmed that gate post at about 20 mph. Ole Mr. Cur dog wasn't paying no never-mind to where he was going and his head hit that corner post with a big thud and a yelp. He then banged against the side of the jeep and got his ass nicked pretty good by the left rear tire. We laughed like hell about that. After that, every time we'd come through there, you could see that son of a bitch sitting way back in the hay barn. All he had in him after that was an occasional and very distant, *woof-woof.*

## Shot in the Tooth

We hunted up there for about a week and on the second or third day, Coonie killed a real nice, long yearling bull elk. When we went to pick him up late that evening, he had the elk right down by the road which I thought was damn convenient. I did notice that the road went right under a little mesa that was straight up above the road. We all got out and I asked Coonie where he had shot him, meaning which area of the ranch, not where in the body.

He grinned and said, "Right up there and in the tooth," pointing straight up. Turns out Kenneth had been ambling along the road, trying to mind his own business, when he heard a noise above him. There peering over the ledge, looking at him was the elk. He unlimbered his trusty 7mm Blunderbuss and let fly at him. The animal immediately disappeared. There was some rustling of brush and leaves, which was the elk wallowing around up there, then the damn thing rolled over the side of the mesa and slid right down to the road. Ken rolled him around to see where he was shot and noticed some blood in his mouth and upon examination, realized he had shot him in the tooth and killed that sucker dead as a hammer, of course.

## Tiny and Big Train

A thousand years ago, back when I was first married and had just come back to the Kyle ranch from our ranch in Mexico, I decided to try and be friends with my brother, Gil. Now, that was gonna take a tad of doing cause Brother Gil and I had seen eye to eye on just about *nuthin* before then.

Brother Gil never really lived at the Buda ranch cause Dad wasn't into nothing that had to do with children. About the first time Brother Gil started talking, which was kinda early, he immediately started asking too damn many questions as far as Dad was concerned. So Dad just upped and shipped his little spindly 8 year old white ass into Austin to live with our grandmother Hamlett, who abided in her little bitty yellow house at 1215 Parkway, just upstream from the Tavern at 12th and Lamar. And, basically, he never came home after that. No wonder he stutters, but we won't go into that.

Anyway, if one was gonna be friends with Brother Gil, one might ask if one could sit with him at the Texas football games, Brother Gil being a T-Man and all. And if one was allowed to join in that very rarefied air, one got to sit on the 50 yard line. Wasn't nothing slouchy about that, either, I'm here to tell you.

Well, Brother Gil *allowed as how* if I could act civilized for just once in my God-damned life, he'd give it some consideration.

Well, fall came as expected, wasn't any surprise there, but the real surprise came when Brother Gil announced that he had given the football thing thorough and thoughtful consideration and that he would *allow* my wife and I to sit with him and his hand picked bunch but only if I would just act right. What ever that meant, cause, it seems I wasn't much into *acting right* before then, least not in Brother Gil's eyes.

So, on the first big home game, we went up and sat right square on the 50 yard line with Brother Gil, Sister Jean and some hand-picked Austin Blue Bloods; hand-picked by Brother Gil, of course. Folks like Bo and Sue Robinson. Only the very best, of course, would do, no put-down intended for my dear friends, Bo and Sue, cause they couldn't help it.

My wife and I sat on the row below Brother Gil, him being above the salt and all, and the game started. Don't know what year it was, but whoever Texas was playing that day just happened to have one of the first Black players in the Southwest Conference on their team which caused Brother Gil no end of consternation.

So, between Brother Gil hollering, *"Kill that black son of a bitch"* and my wife asking all who would listen, "How come all those nice boys down there were kicking that little oblong little ball up and down that pretty grass field?" Things kinda went to shit in a hand-basket for me. I kept feeling in my pockets to see if I had brought any tequila with me. Cause if I had, I was gonna partake of about a quart of it, and perhaps, just perhaps, revert back to my real self , which probably would have embarrassed the dog-shit out of Brother Gil, one, and two, gotten me ejected from the game. And, it was only my first attempt in a long time at being *civilized*. Damn, I was losing my touch.

Well, somebody won, but I was so steamed at Brother Gil, I didn't give a shit who. I think we went to one more game when my wife finally said she was tired of trying to figure out *"why all those wonderful college boys were acting so mean to one another,"* so she quit going. At the same time, I figured being *civilized* wasn't my style and I might as well have a conversion.

Turns out Providence was at hand! Texas was scheduled to play Oklahoma State or some team that had another Black player and an idea descended down to me from *ABOVE* that I thought might work. So, I called Cactus Pryor and asked him if he knew two nice black boys who would like to sit on the 50 yard line of the up-coming game. He said he didn't, but to call John Henry Faulk. Well, I called John Henry and he couldn't help me either, but he said, "Why don't you called your dear ole Coonie, maybe he can help."

Well, I called Coonie the next day and told him my plan and asked him if he could help and he said, "Well, you know what, I just happen to have Tiny and Big Train working in the kitchen at Green Pastures. Let me ask them if they would like to go."

## The Plan

Turns out Tiny and Big Train told Coonie they'd love to, so I hopped in my truck and went over to Green Pastures to interview the Christians on their way to the Coliseum.

*Shit.* Those were two of the biggest, blackest sons a bitches I ever saw, no disrespect intended. Both must have been 6-4 to 6-6 and weighed north of 285 pounds a piece. I very politely told both of them what I was trying to do and what they were getting themselves into. They got the biggest grins on their faces you ever saw, said, not to worry, they could probably handle it. Handle it, shit, they probably could've whipped everyone in that whole part of the stadium, and thrown in Brother Gil just for good measure.

I gave them our two tickets and fifty dollars. I told them to dress up in suits and ties and buy some of those funky hats and flags that are from the opposing team, and, oh, one other thing. Wait until the kickoff happens and the instant it does, walk out of the stadium stairwell and go up to your seats. They grinned again, and said, "Thank you, no problem." Those boys were good at instruction. Both probably are corporate heads of some fancy companies by now.

Well, the game came and went. Knowing my Brother Gil as well as I did and also knowing he had a enough loose screws rattling around in him that he would hire somebody to come over and burn my fucking house down, I was a tad nervous. So, from that

Saturday plumb through the balance of the next week, I paced the floor of my house on Ridgewood Road in Rolling Wood waiting. Nothing. Shit!

The phone finally rang late Sunday afternoon 8 days later and I nervously answered it. The voice exploded from the other end: "*You did it. We know damn well you did it. Don't deny it cause we know you did it!*" All the while laughing and howling in delight. It was Sue Robinson. Shit! Caught! "What do you mean?" I stuttered. See Brother Gil isn't the only one who lived with my father long enough to learn how to stutter.

Well, here be the skinny: Seems that on the way up the ramp to get to their seats, Bo and Sue walked right by two very nicely dressed rather large black men, who as Sue said, must have been professional football players here to enjoy the game. They went on up and sat down in their prescribed special seats provided by Brother Gil. When all of a sudden, the same two rather large gentlemen exited the ramp hole below them and started up in their direction. Sue poked Bo in the ribs and said, "*Lookee, there are those two enormous black men we just saw, and they are coming this way, and Bo, they be turning in our row, and Bo, they be sitting right here beside us.*"

Well, Brother Gil was not paying attention and all of a sudden two very large, very black men sat down directly in front of him and he damn near shit an Elgin/Butler brick. He very nervously reached over and tapped Big Train on the back and said, "You be sitting in the wrong seats" at which time Big Train simply held up his hand containing the two tickets which stated the correct seat numbers.

Sue told me later she had never in her whole life seen Brother Gil quite so subdued. Needless to say, Brother Gil did not succumb to his normal self of hollering, "*Kill those black sons a bitches,*" during that particular ball game.

## Banished Forever

For some reason, our season football tickets were revoked and we unable to sit among the *unwashed* ever again. Bless Coonie's heart. I will never be able to repay him for that fabulous service. And above all, my endearing thanks to Tiny and Big Train, where ever they may be.

## What It's All About

Ken Koock and I have been friends and family forever. Betty and I were invited to his 76th birthday celebration recently. We laughed and hugged each other as we reiterated; "Once a Coonie, always a Coonie!"

**Cactus Pryor and MEK**

# Richard "Cactus" Pryor

## Austin, Texas
## 1923–2011

Austin was not a very big town when we were growing up and everyone knew everyone else. Even though our ranch was in Hays County west of Buda, Mother and Dad did all their socializing in Austin. They were members of the Austin Country Club, the Austin Dance Club, etc. and everywhere one went in those days, one would always bump into and be friends with Richard Cactus Pryor.

Cactus had been in the radio business since the 1940s when he went to work for the Johnson's at their radio station in Austin. He was one of those special individuals who was funny as hell and could think on his feet. Over the years he became a natural as a speaker for special events around the state.

He had his own radio show in Austin for years and would invite all sorts of folks to be his guest. One of his favorite guests was my father. When Cactus first started the show most of the interviews were live, that is until my father showed up. The first interview Cactus ever did with Dad, everything was fine until Cactus asked Dad what he thought about trespassers, one of Dad's pet peeves. Dad reared back in his chair and hollered; "Why, all those no good sons a bitches ought to be shot," and then really started cussing. Cactus told me later, he nearly broke his arm grabbing the *off* switch on the microphone Dad was using. Needless to say, after that Cactus always taped Dad so he could bleep him, just to be on the safe side.

## Speaking Tours

Cactus was in big demand for speaking events held by the Chambers of Commerce, Lions Clubs etc. His routine was always the same in that he would always go in character and he was hilarious. He would go as a Danish Prince; a Mexican General; you name it and he would do it, and, always in costume, medals and all.

What most folks didn't know, Cactus was as bald as a billiard and he always wore a toupee. Sometimes, he would show up as a bald Norwegian Count in the afternoon and that night, he would put on his toupée and come out on stage as himself, or any combination that he wanted.

He asked me to fly him on some of these outings and the funniest one I remember was when we flew down to Corpus Christi, Texas so he could be the speaker at the annual gala for the local Chamber of Commerce. He had arranged a ride back home the next day, so I dropped him off and returned to Austin. Here's how the story unfolded.

## Prince Charming

Cactus told the President of the Chamber to put out the word that a Danish Prince was going to be the speaker that evening, but beforehand, the Prince would like to purchase some "wonderful cows" from a local farmer that he could ship back to his farm in Denmark as a reminder of his marvelous stay in Texas.

The Chamber President met the airplane and whisked Cactus off to a nearby hotel where he could change into his regalia. He emerged in full uniform with its 900 medals attached, etc.

When the word got out that a possible purchase of cows was in the offing, the local county judge, *allowed as how*, he "just happened" to have about 25 prime heifers that, if the price was right, he could be persuaded to sell; knowing full well, that perhaps, just perhaps, there was indeed a God in Heaven and that a pigeon was coming to Jim Wells County, Texas. A pigeon that could be clipped.

Well, Cactus, whoops, I mean Prince Charming of Denmark, exited the hotel in the full uniform of a possible Danish Prince, sporting his best dark toupee, and as an added bonus, a wonderful handlebar mustache. He was immediately picked up by the Chamber fellow and the county judge *hisself*.

## The Purchase

They drove out to the edge of town to the judge's farm where the judge just happened to have his 25 prime heifers in a set of corrals all ready for inspection. They all exited the vehicle and proceeded to show the Prince around the place, when they came upon the corral full of the cattle in question. Cactus asked if those were the wonderful Texas cows that could be bought and the friendly judge replied, "Indeed."

At that point in the charade, Cactus pulled out the perfumed handkerchief he kept in his pocket for just such rare occasions, stepped up on the edge of the corral fence, waved the hankie around in the air for a moment, he pointed it at the particular cows in question and a very poor Danish accent, (that, of course, no one recognized nor gave a shit about) and proclaimed, "*They are mine! Ship those lovely creatures to my little 10,000-acre farm in Denmark, if you please.*"

Pleased! The judge was so pleased he damn near passed a Bois-de-arc ball right then and there. Then, just as they stepped away from the corral fence, the judge's little ten year old son came hippy-hopping up with his collie dog at his side. Without missing a beat, Cactus pointed his little perfumed hankie at the boy's dog and said, "*Him too, if you please,*" meaning, of course, the little boy's dog. Well, the judge stuttered, just for a moment, and nodded his approval.

With that, the little boy started howling his head off so the judge quickly had him ushered into the house. Cactus told me later, you could have heard the little boy squalling for a mile.

## Le Coup De Grace

Now comes the good part. That night Cactus walked out on the stage as a Prince from Denmark to give his speech. He started his talk on how wonderful it was to be in the great Province of Texas and noted how marvelous the local official had been to sell him all those wonderful Texas animals, all the while in his fake Danish accent. As he did, he began to remove his mustache and his toupee and by the time he finished removing the entire disguise, he was talking with a full blown Texas accent as Cactus Pryor from Austin, Texas, and "*Good God All Mighty,*" how pleased he was to be there.

Well, the story then goes on to reflect that one County Judge in question was last seen crawling out of those particular annual festivities on his hands and knees, hoping never to be seen in that County again.

Cactus was one of those rare, good folks that come flying by once in a millennium. What a pleasure it was for me and my family to be standing close as he passed by.

MEK and Cliff Logan

# Cliff K. Logan
## Austin, Texas

**C**ousin Cliff. Cliff's mother had a Kuykendall hidden in her family tree back in Bell County history somewhere and when we found out about it we declared ourselves cousins and cousins it's been ever since.

I've always dabbled in antique guns between the droughts in my life. Cousin has been in the general antique business ever since he worked for Raymond Brown at the Country Store Gallery at 14th and Lavaca in Austin, and somehow lived to tell the tale. It was there that Cliff got to meet everyone in Texas who wanted to buy a piece of art.

When Cliff branched out of his own, he started attending all the major art and gun shows in Santa Fe, Tulsa, Denver, Phoenix and beyond, and very soon became one of the most well known and reputable art dealers in the southwest. Not an easy task in the rough and tumble arena of that industry but after some 30-40 years of doing it, he stands today at the very top of his game.

He continues to surprise me with his acquisitions of rare art, old guns, presentation saddles etc. I'm always asking him how he does it. He laughs and says; "Well, after 100 years or so of working 24 hours a days, 7 days a week, the word has finally gotten around that I am the person to call if an individual, or a museum, has something they wish to get rid of or sell."

## A Case in Point

Several years ago a woman walked into a major Texas museum carrying a cardboard box and asked for the curator. The curator showed up and asked how she might be able to help the woman. The lady then said she had something that had belonged to her great-grandfather that she would like to sell to the museum because she needed the money.

At that point, the curator invited her into the main office and said; "Let me see what you have in the box." Any antique items that pertain to the Texas Revolution, to the Civil War, or to the trail driving days are items that cause a tremendous amount of interest. But, if a Texas Ranger item shows up, it gets everyone's attention in a hurry. Well, Pilgrim, let me tell you what she had.

The lady took the lid off of the box and began to unwrap what turned out to be an 1844 Walker 44 Colt percussion revolver, in its original Slim-Jim holster. It had Texas proofs, paper work, and pictures of her great-grandfather holding the gun from after the Civil War. It just so happens that he had ridden with Jack Hays and his original Ranger Company into Mexico during the War of 1846. The curator was obliged to sit down for a moment just to get her breath.

The curator asked the woman what she wanted for the gun. The figure she quoted was substantial. She then asked the women to leave the items with her in the museum and told her she would get back to her ASAP.

As soon as the woman walked out of the museum, the curator picked up the phone, dialed Cliff's number in Austin, and told him what had just transpired. With no hesitation, Cliff said, "I'll take it. Call the woman back and tell her it is sold."

Cliff told me later it was one of the most important items he ever acquired in an entire lifetime of collecting.

## Another Opportunity

Not long after the Walker Colt acquisition, a woman called Cliff from west Texas to tell him she had some of her great grandfather's stuff, told him what it was. She asked him if he would he like to come look at it. Cliff said he threw his sandwich down on the floor for his bird dog to eat, grabbed his over-night bag and out the door he went.

Turns out the woman's great grandfather was a Texas Ranger in the Frontier Battalion before 1900. Cliff met the woman in west Texas and she took him down to her storage unit where all the "loot" was located. Cliff said when she opened the unit all he saw was box after box of stuff. Seems the old Ranger had never thrown anything away, and neither had his family for over 100 years. The storage unit had all his paper files; all kinds of photos; every "Fugitive from Justice" book he had ever carried; his six shooter in its holster; his rifle in its scabbard; his handcuffs; even his bowie knife.

Again, it was just about the finest Texas Ranger material collected in past 75 years. I will tell you this, Cousin has quite a nose for sniffing stuff out and the good news is; he knows what it is when he sees it. No one is better.

## On to Denver

I try and make the Colorado Gun Collectors show each May in Denver. He sets up there and always has a bunch of tables full of wonderful contraband. Many times Enrique Guerra and his son, Che, (José) from the Texas Rio Grande Valley will be there with him. We all make it a point to supper-up each night at some fabulous Denver night spot and talk about the rare guns we either bought or just missed.

Che Guerra

## On to Santa Fe

Cousin also goes to Santa Fe every August for all the major art and antique shows. We all gather up at least once for a good visit and try and figure out some new and wonderful place to dine.

Those are special times for us. As we say goodnight, Cliff always turns to us and says; "Let me know if there is anything I can do for either one of you."

*Cousin, you just did.*

**Bill Peace, Cliff Logan and MEK**

Enrique E. Guerra

# Enrique E. Guerra

## San Vicente Ranch, Linn, Texas

If there ever was a person who was south Texas Vaquero royalty, it is Enrique E. Guerra, owner of the San Vicente Ranch near Linn, Texas. His family has been ranching on the Frontera of northern Mexico and present day south Texas since about two days after Cortez whipped up on Montezuma. The San Vicente ranch is a part of the original Nueva Santander Grant and the Santa Anita Land Grant, both date back to the 1750s.

Enrique comes from that old school where manners and graciousness were integral with ones daily life and to be otherwise for him would be unseemly. Whenever I see him, I am obliged to stand for a moment and show him the respect that he deserves and I do so with a great deal of pleasure.

I met Enrique in the 1950's at a Texas Gun Collectors show in San Antonio that David Allen and I were attending. Not only is he a well known south Texas rancher, but he is known in collector circles as having one of the finest private collection of antique firearms representing northern Mexico and south Texas in existence.

Betty's mother was living in the Rio Grande Valley. Enrique told me if we ever came that way that we must stop by his ranch for a visit. Turns out, we decided to make a run down there (The Texas Rio Grande Valley is down there) on an Easter Saturday morning. As we went through San Antonio, I called Enrique on my fancy car phone and he told me it was perfect timing; that the house was full of kids and kin-folks, and he needed a break. He asked about what time we'd be there, and told me he'd meet us at his front gate of the San Vicente.

Sure enough, when we got there at about 11 o'clock, Enrique was sitting in his truck at the main entrance reading his paper and told us to follow him. We caravanned down to his headquarters, which was a flat-roofed hacienda with large courtyard in front completely filled with yucca, palm, and other plants indigenous to deep south Texas. We piled out of our vehicles and went into the hacienda through some massive carved wooden Mexican double doors and stepped into his great room; "Sala de Estar."

The living room was good sized and completely furnished with ranch and family heirlooms dating back 150 years. The walls were covered with oil paintings of Spanish Noblemen in armor that must have been ten feet tall in their frames. Over on the far side of the room were very early presentation, silver-mounted Charro Saddles that had belonged to different presidents and governors of Mexico. It was a dazzling display to say the least.

## La Comida

About that time there was a loud holler from la Cocinera that "la comida" was ready. Knowing that we were intruding on his Easter weekend, just by stopping by, Betty and I immediately began to say our Graces and try to leave. Enrique in typical gracious fashion, simply said, "Nonsense." We filed into the dining room and were immediately seated with Enrique's lovely wife, Lydia, and about six or eight siblings and their wives while la Cocinera, and others, brought in the most scrumptious vittles known to mankind. Betty and I were very blessed that day to be able to enjoy the company of such a lovely family.

After lunch, Enrique gave us a tour of the hacienda, noting in this room and that, the marvelous antiques and heirlooms from generations past of his family in south Texas. We finally were able to say, adios, about mid-afternoon and proceed on our way. The warmness of that visit has stuck in our minds to this day.

His son, Ché Guerra, and my 19th cousin 12 times removed, Cliff Logan, are big buddies in southwestern art, paintings, Charro saddles, and western memorabilia. The two of them attend most of the major art and gun collector shows in the southwest every year and Enrique is usually with them. And, since Cousin Cliff has invited me to some of them over the past 10–15 years, I have had the distinct pleasure of being able to break bread and sip some mighty good whiskey with that fine south Texas gentleman.

We are both getting a tad long in the tooth, his tooth being slightly longer than mine, and our visits are not as often now as I would like. Maybe we'll get another chance for one more sip or two down the dusty road, who knows? What a pleasure that would be.

He loves nature in spite of
what it did to him.

—Forrest Tucker

Bo Robinson III

# George Edward "Bo" Robinson III

## Austin, Texas
## 1938–1978

The Robinsons and the Kuykendalls have been tied together ever since grandfather Gill bought the 11,000-acre 101 Ranch at Buda in 1901. The Robinsons own the 8,000-acre+/- ranch in north Austin, known as Austin White Lime. Their ranch used to be way north of Austin at the village of McNeil. Now, McNeil and the ranch are smack dab in the middle of Austin. Damn, what a dilemma?

When I was growing up there were three siblings; Al, George, Flora (Sis) and their mother, Mrs. Alfred Bremond Robinson, better known as Mama Al, and a bunch of little Robinsons running around all over west Austin. Somewhere in that bunch was George "Bo" Robinson.

Sis Robinson and my father were big buddies as far back as I can remember. Sis loved to hunt as much as my Dad did. She was out at the 101 Ranch messing around all the time and every now and then, she'd haul out one or two of those little sandy-headed monsters with her. That's when I became life-long friends with Bo, and his sister Patricia, both children of Papa George. Sis had no children of her own.

### Birthdays

My particular family is especially joined with Bo's bunch cause all my children were delivered by their uncle, Dr. James Eckardt, and all were born on the same day. GeorgeAnn, Bo's first child, was born on the 28th of December in one room, and Marshall Jr. was born 30 minutes later in the joining room. Old Dr. Eckardt was busy as a one armed paper-hanger pulling on both of those little rascals and GeorgeAnn popped out first.

Then a year and a half later, my daughter Mary Alice was born on April 20th, which was Mama Al Robinson's birthday. Ten months and thirty two seconds later, my daughter Sarita was born on May the 8th. One year later, on the same day, Little George Robinson would be born to Bo and Sue. Talk about spooky. Shit! Tell me about it?

Bo and Little George

## A Big Hunting Clan

In later years, Dad and I had hunted with Raleigh Ross on part of the Bowman ranch at Big Wells. When we finished with it, the Robinson clan leased the same 10,000 acre pasture and kept it for many years. The Robinsons were all a big hunting family and had been all of their lives. If they were not hunting in south Texas, then off to Africa they would go, all in a bunch. The adventure of the hunting chase, no matter where, ran deeply in all their blood, especially in Bo and Spike. They were with-out a doubt wild game hunters extraordinaire!

Bo and guide, Jacarilla Indian Reservation

When we were all growing up, most folks thought that Bo and Spike Robinson were brothers, because they were always together, but in fact they were 1st cousins. Bo was the son of George E. Robinson and Spike was the son of George's brother, Alfred H. Robinson. Bo was three years older than Spike. Spike's real name was Alfred H. Robinson III, which he never used. He was always just Spike to everyone he knew. He did have one other name, however; Bo called him "*Sparkle*."

**Sue, Bo, Sis and Bill**

It was this pair of cousins that were my good friends and also the same bunch that I had introduced Bill Peace to earlier. It was also this pair that got us into so much trouble that special night at the Poso Ranch at El Vado, NM a thousand years ago, when they made us drink all that sorry whiskey and the owner of the establishment got mad at Bill for fucking up his knife.

**Bo, Spike and other rowdies**

## The End of the Dusty Road

Life kinda changed after that. Bo's life had been in somewhat of a turmoil for a while and he went up to spend the night at Bill Peace's place on Lake Travis to visit and to see if he could sort things out. Bill told me later, they stayed up most of the night talking. The next morning, Bo called me from there and said they were coming down to my place at Appaloosa Run to see me and for me to wait for them.

They never made it. They were in two cars with Bill in the lead and when Bill turned into Appaloosa Run, he looked behind him in the rear view mirror and noticed that Bo had pulled off on the shoulder on FM 1826. Bill turned around and went back to see what was the matter and as he passed Bo's car, he could see he was slumped over in the front seat.

What ever knots Bo had tied in his string came undone that day. Seems life suddenly got too heavy for my dear friend, so he stopped his car, stuck his 22 Magnum pistol in his ear and touched it off.

Several days later, the Robinson family took Bo up to the private family grave plot in the middle of their ranch at McNeil and buried him there. Just about all of Old Austin attended.

## Things Got Different

Things were never quite the same after that, but that is the way it was. Folks need to understand there are some things you can't take back, no matter how hard you wish you could. When the string of life that you have been holding on to forever suddenly starts to unravel, you are pretty much done.

I don't think about Bo now as much as I used to, but when I do, I can't help but get a big smile on my face as some of those fine memories pour through my mind. We were not kin, but we were close enough to be hugging cousins and I figure that's about as fine as it gets.

In my minds eye I can see him and Bill Peace sitting together on a big termite mound in the middle of the Serengeti Plain glassing a big full-mane lion and grinning like they had good sense. They feel my presence and both lean back and wave at me, "*Come on, what are you waiting for?*"

I wave back, "*Not yet fellas, not just yet!*"

**My Old Friend**

**They had all the vices I admired and none of the virtues I abhorred.**

—Winston Churchill

Mewes, Bill Goetzmann and MEK

# William H. "Bill" Goetzmann, PhD

## Austin, Texas
## 1930–2010

**B**ill Goetzmann; A Pulitzer-Winning Historian; Teacher; Professor; Philosopher; Story-teller; friend; and on top of all that, just about the finest left-handed fencer to ever come out of Yale University.

He and his wife, Mewes, have been our friends since the early 1960s. In those early days most all the roads in West Lake were gravel. Many University of Texas Professors had found the hills just west of down-town Austin to be a perfect hide-away haven.

Somehow, we all found one another and many a night was spent over some fine sipping whiskey cussing and discussing everything known to man and beast.

**Bill (center) Team Captain**

### The Mountain Men

By the time we first met, Bill had already written his book Exploration and Empire, which won him the Pulitzer. He knew all there was to be known in the whole world about the American West. It didn't matter whether the discussion was about Lewis and Clark; Fremont; Kit Carson; the Oregon Trail; the Military Mapping of the West; Sacagawea; or Coulter's great run from Three Points on the Missouri River to the mouth of the Yellowstone; Bill knew every single detail.

Many early European noblemen traveled out west to rummage among the mountain men in the 1820s and 30s. Just about each one had included his own artist or secretary to record, sketch and paint the moment. Bill knew the location of every item, painting, sketch, drawing, no matter where in the world it was located. He spent years researching all of them here and in Europe. I don't doubt he got permission from all the museums and individuals to not only view them, but even touch them so he could get a feel for them to write about.

Several of the museums in St. Louis, Tulsa and Cody, Wyoming have many of the diaries of the few mountain men who could read and write. Bill told me he had researched and read every single one of them.

## The Buffalo Bill Museum, Cody, Wyoming

Bill was on the board of the Buffalo Bill Museum at Cody, Wyoming, and one year he invited me to go with him up there for a seminar. We flew into Billings; one can't get into Cody directly without difficulty. As we were driving our rental car down from Montana towards Cody, Bill would single out place after place where a Mountain Man had done this or some Sioux or Crow Indian had done that. It was quite a history lesson.

We arrived at Cody and while he was busy with museum business, I tried to tour the museum. I say tried, because it is immense. It would take three or four days of looking and prowling to do it justice. Not only does it house all of Buffalo Bill's stuff; it has every known Indian item; complete teepee villages; Frederick Remington's office and studio; the entire Winchester Arms Collection, that had been moved from Connecticut; and ten million other displays. It was mind boggling. Anyone who has an interest in the American West must go there. What an enjoyable time we had together.

## Then There Was the Wedding

He and Mewes invited me up to their daughter Ann's wedding in New Haven, Connecticut back in "Ought 3," hell, I can't remember. But I do remember that I got to ride on the airship with one of Mewes's five good looking sisters, all who live in and around Houston.

We got to stay at the famous Yale Tennis Club facility which had been built way before WW I and those damn Yankees up there had never heard of air conditioning. Shit, it was hot! Me and Mewes's sister got up in the middle of the night (No we had not been staying together) and hauled our damn bed sheets down to the only bathroom in the fucking facility, stood in the shower with them wrapped around us, and then went back to bed. It got worse. It was miserable!

That following evening there was a wedding rehearsal party in someone's house and I drank just about all the whiskey I could find in New Haven, West Haven, South

Haven and North Haven and in doing so ended up trying to gently remove all the clothes off of a very good looking bridesmaid, who as it turns out, was not a bridesmaid at all, but simply a guest from down the street. For some reason she was not a happy camper over it all, but I don't know why. Damn, sometimes people just get huffy over anything.

## The Yale Yacht Club

Bill swung by the Tennis Club just before lunch to take me to the Yale Club to get a bite to eat. Now mind you, everything around there was a "Club." Yale Club, Yacht Club, Rowing Club, Alumni Club: Those damn Yale-ites were chock full of going to some sort of Club.

Anyway, Bill drug me into the Yale Club where all these real narrow 20 to 30 foot canoes were hanging from the ceiling. Must have been a hundred of them; so damn narrow that your butt wouldn't fit on any of them. Wouldn't be worth a shit on Onion Creek trying to catch a perch, and, man, there must have been 10,000 pictures of classmates in their striped T-shirts from way back before the turn of the century. It was also the same club where the Wiffenpoofs sang their song, whoever they were. Thank God they weren't singing it that day

Didn't matter to me very much; however, I was so damn hung-over from all that fine whiskey the night before that I barely remember being there and whatever history Bill imparted to me about that place has been lost to time and damaged brain cells.

We got Ann married off to someone that afternoon and I think I had a good time.

## Lasting Memories

Bill's mind was like a steel trap, or perhaps a great black hole in the universe that captured and retained any information that even got close. While he looked like the rumpled professor type, with his blue blazer pockets stuffed with pencils and notes, there was nothing rumpled about him at all. And, on top of everything, he was funny as hell.

For over fifty years, we did everything together, birthdays, Christmas, Thanksgiving, graduations, marriages, divorces, travel, you name it and we have done it together.

As I enter the winter of my life and attempt to recall those memories of seasons past, my friendship with Bill and Mewes Goetzmann stands out as one of those wonderful accomplishments that very few people on this particular planet are allowed to enjoy.

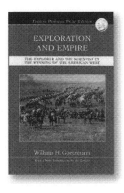

### Bill Knew All There Was to Know in the Whole World and Mark Twain Might Have Known the Rest

Bill & M. F. Johnson

# Bill and M. F. Johnson
## Wimberley, Texas

Just stepping into the O'Neil Ford designed 1940s ranch home on the banks of Cypress Creek in Wimberley, Texas sets the stage for one of the most remarkable encounters one could have in twelve lifetimes. You can hear the lilt of the wonderful voices of Bill and M. F. as they spin the fabulous tales of the Texas Hill Country. The aroma of all the food in the kitchen cooked for the evening spills over you from the slight breeze sweeping through the open windows of this magnificent place. The very telling of it causes goose bumps to appear all over me and makes me want to bolt out the door and head down that way to see and hug my two old friends.

I had met his father and mother first. William Parks Johnson, known as "Parks" and his lovely wife, Joyce Louise Johnson, known as Louise, were old friends of my aunt Dorothy, Dad's sister. They lived down along Cypress Creek in the center of Wimberley on land that had belonged to Louise's family since the 1920's. Louise's bunch of Johnson's was well known San Marcos and Wimberley folks that had been friends of the Kuykendalls since we moved to Hays County in 1901.

Bill's father, Parks, was very well known for having been involved in early radio and a radio program called "VOX POP." One night in 1932, while working for KTRH

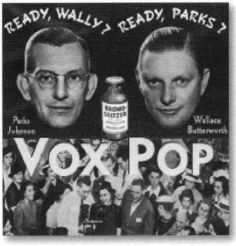

**Vox Pop**

Radio in Houston, Parks decided to take a microphone out on the street to question passer-bys about the upcoming presidential election between Hoover and Roosevelt.

The response was so great that Parks was able to expand the program of *off the cuff* street interviews into what was to be labeled "VOX POP," or "Voice of the People."

The series came to an end in 1948 and between 1932 and that closing date, Parks Johnson and his co-hosts visited 41 states and 6 foreign countries.

## WWII

Bill Johnson was enrolled at the University of Texas at Austin when WWII started and he decided he might as well uphold the family tradition as Indian fighters and frontiersman and get into the fight as soon as he could. So, he upped and joined the US Marine Corp, got his commission as a 2nd Louie, and then got his skinny white butt shipped out just in time to make the invasion on Iwo Jima. As he told me one time; "Good timing means everything."

He also told me that 15 or 20 Second Lieutenants were killed or wounded in the first few days of fighting which, as he said, "...allowed him the golden opportunity to view the Island first hand."

## Mt. Suribachi

Bill was on Iwo Jima and able to witness the American Flag been raised on Mt. Suribachi just before a Jap bullet nearly took off his hand. He was shipped to the Island of Guam where the American hospital was located and after much surgery to save most of his hand, returned state side.

He then renewed his University of Texas studies, graduating in 1946.

## The Get Together

Mary Frances Brown, better known to the whole world as M. F., comes from a pretty fancy family of aviators who knew just about everyone in the old days who could flap their wings. Folks like someone named Amelia and a one-eyed fellow named Wiley, who just by chance decided to fly his airship into a mountain in Alaska. The only problem with that was he decided to take Will Rogers with him.

M. F. had her own airplane for a while, was a model for the Powers Modeling Agency in Dallas, and attended one of the first radio and TV classes at UT, and I think was possibly interviewed by Parks Johnson for VOX POP radio while there. Parks took one look at this tall, good looking drink of water, and said, "You know, M. F., I might just know a long, tall, skinny, ex-US Marine that you would like to meet." And therein lays the best part of this tale.

## Neighbors

Since our ranch was located not far from theirs, our paths have crossed back and forth for the last 50 to 60 years. I remember one time, when I was over at the other ranch visiting my crazy cousin, Worth, and my Aunt Dorothy. Bill and M. F. were there talking to Aunt Dot about moving an ancient log cabin from inside the corrals over to their place in Wimberley. Seems they wanted to create some sort of compound near Cypress Creek and the log cabin at the old Kuykendall 101 ranch headquarters might work.

I asked Bill about it later and he laughed and said; "Oh, I was just helping Dorothy get the durn thing out of the corral but it was pretty much rotted and we could only use a few of the logs."

If there ever was a Mr. and Mrs. Wimberley it is this pair. From Camp Longhorn on Inks Lake to the Devils Backbone at Wimberley; they have made their indelible mark on this area of the Texas Hill Country. Many a time, Betty and I have been invited to their wonderful home for an evening of story telling, great vittles and better company.

*Nothing wrong with that!*

**Bill & M. F.**

Michael Frary

# Michael Frary
# Artist Extraordinaire
## Austin, Texas
## 1918–2005

**M**y old friend, Michael Frary, was born in California, but as he said, "he moved to Texas just as soon as he could afford it." His father died when he was an infant and family members moved him to Florida. In time he graduated from Palm Beach High School. Immediately after that, he moved back to California, and being a talented swimmer, was offered a swimming scholarship to attend the University of Southern California. He soon became a champion swimmer and was captain of the USC varsity water polo team. While there, he earned eight sporting letters, the most offered at the school at that time. He graduated in 1940 with a Bachelor degree in Architecture and obtained a Master of Fine Arts degree the following year.

Michael joined the US Navy and at the conclusion of the war in 1945, he went to work as assistant art director for Goldwyn Studios, Paramount and finally Universal Studios. The life working for the studios did not give him time to paint so he started teaching night classes in painting, when UCLA beckoned and offered him a full time teaching job.

## Later

In the early 1950s, Michael was offered a job in San Antonio to work for Marion Koogler McNay. It was during his time there that he met Peggy Chittenden Mathewson. They were married shortly thereafter.

Then in 1952, he was offered a job as assistant professor with the University of Texas. In 1970, the University named him Professor of Art. When he retired in 1986, he was named Professor Emeritus of Art.

Over his many years of teaching and painting, Michael received nearly 200 awards and was in as many one man shows across the country. His half century of work also produced three books: *Impressions of the Big Thicket*, UT Press, 1973; *Impressions of the Texas Panhandle*, Texas A&M Press, 1977; and *Watercolors of the Rio Grande*, Texas A&M Press, 1984.

## First Meeting

I met Michael and Peggy Frary after I had moved back from the Mexican ranch to our ranch in Hays County. We met, not because I am the living authority on art, but because he and Peggy threw the most fun parties in Austin, Texas. He and Peggy loved to talk about Texas, Texas History and Texas ranching. We hit it off the first time we got together.

So, from about 1965 on, we all got together as much as we could, either at their house in Austin or at one of my places. Every time we did, Michael would eat my ass out about how sorry my art was and questioned when was I gonna get some "real" art to hang on my walls instead of all that western crap. I loved it and so did he. In later years we got a watercolor or two from him and made sure they were hanging on the wall in a prominent place every time he and Peggy came to our house. He thrived on giving me a hard time about my total lack of knowledge on anything to do with art and I loved his humor.

Then in 2002, as a present on my 70th birthday, Michael painted me a portrait of the renowned rancher and Texas pioneer, Charles Goodnight, and told me it better be hanging up in my house the next time he showed up. It was and it is. He got a big charge out of that. It is a fabulous work of art.

## The British Addition

One cannot say a word about Michael without throwing in fourteen pages about Peggy. She is the most regal person I have ever been around, except of course my mother.

What I know about Peggy comes from bits and pieces I have picked up over all these years. Seems she was married in the late 30s or early 1940s, to a RAF pilot who was subsequently killed in the Battle of Britain. It is my understanding that she in the British Army as a lorry driver during the horribly time of the blitz. In January of 1945, she married Christy Mathewson, Jr, whose father was a Hall of Fame baseball pitcher from before WWI. Peggy's name in the records at the time was Lola Finch. Christy Jr. was a well known aviator, having flown in China in the early 1930's. He was promoted to Lieutenant Colonel in the US Army Air Corp and was posted to London as a liaison officer with the Air Transport Command. That is where he and Peggy met.

He was discharged from the service in 1946. He and Peggy moved to San Antonio, Texas and they bought a ranch NW of there near Helotes, Texas. In the summer of 1950, Christy was in the house alone when a gas explosion occurred and he was terribly burned over his entire body. He died the next day in a San Antonio hospital. He was only 43 years old.

## The Celebration

I was at their house in the summer of 1979, which just so happened to be the upcoming 40th anniversary of the Battle of Britain (September 1939–1979). England was going to throw a tremendous celebration for all the veterans who participated in the battle and have everyone in full regalia, medals and all. All of which was going to culminate in everyone being in Westminster Abbey for the finale. I told Peggy what an honor that would be just to be there and witness history first hand. She turned to me and said; "Well, you must go then, and while there, I will see to it that you are the guest of my uncle, who just so happens to be the Minister of the Abbey!"

There are a few things I regret not doing in the this life and not going to England and staying on the Westminster Abbey grounds as guest of Peggy Chittenden Frary's uncle for this particular event is definitely one of them.

## His Memorial

Michael died in late August of 2005 and Peggy asked me if I would say a few words at his memorial. Even though I have a tendency to stutter when speaking publicly, I immediately accepted.

There were three or four others who spoke before I did and they went on and on about Michaels life-time contribution to the art world. Well, I knew I was dead right there, cause I don't know shit from *Shinola* about art, no pun intended. Then it occurred to me that was exactly what Mike would like for me to say. So, after all the others had finished, I got up to the microphone, struggled for a moment, and started.

"Here I am speaking after all these fine folks who know all there is to know in the whole world about art; who are memorializing a man who also knew everything about the subject and I don't know a thing about it. I'm up here because Michael Frary was my good friend, who loved Texas ranching and hunting stories, and who loved to give me hell every time he could about how sorry my pieces of western art were that I had hanging on my wall."

Everyone laughed; Peggy was pleased and I felt like I had dodged another bullet. Miss those good times we all had together over so many years. Good things will sometimes change and that's the nature of a *dusty road*.

# Epilogue

My friends around the coffee shop are bitching and moaning that I didn't put them in my new book of "Extraordinary" people. Well, guess what, I have been taping most of our conversations about "Secret Sex in our Younger Years" and Scott, Terry, Bill, David, Nick and Paul... you are next. Better start looking for a hole, 'cause you're gonna need one. GOD, it's gonna be great!

In the meanwhile, all the best to you and yours.
—Marshall

# Photo Album

Ken, Bill and MEK, Jr.

Betty and MEK

Sis Robinson King

MEK ROTC Camp, 1954

Cactus and Raleigh

Oscar, James, Big George and Bo

MEK, Jr. and MEK, Sr.

Kyle High School 60th

General LeMay

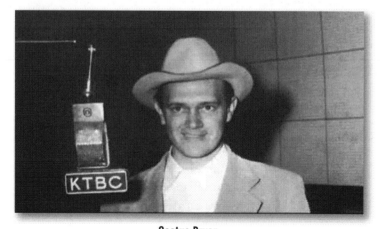

Cactus Pryor

Bill Goetzmann

Betty and MEK

Joe Ely and MEK

**Bill Peace and MEK**

**Alan Lomax**

**Robert Ryan**

**Captain Frank Hamer**

Bill, Bobbie and Bo

David L. Allen, Llama Judge

MEK and Dean Kilgore

Bill Peace

"You got that?" —MEK

Made in the USA
Columbia, SC
07 February 2022

55625462R00083